LAURENCE STERNE:
Riddles and Mysteries

LAURENCE STERNE:
Riddles and Mysteries

edited by
Valerie Grosvenor Myer

VISION
and
BARNES & NOBLE

Vision Press Limited
Fulham Wharf
Townmead Road
London SW6 2SB

and

Barnes & Noble Books
81 Adams Drive
Totowa, NJ 07512

ISBN (UK) 0 85478 445 4
ISBN (US) 0 389 20473 0

**For
Joe Bennett**

Printed and bound in Great Britain by
Unwin Brothers Ltd.,
Old Woking, Surrey.
Phototypeset by Galleon Photosetting,
Ipswich, Suffolk.
MCMLXXXIV

Contents

Contents

Part Four: AFTERWORD

Introduction

by VALERIE GROSVENOR MYER

'The best Book, that has been writ by any Englishman these
thirty Years . . . is *Tristram Shandy*, bad as it is', wrote David
Hume in 1773. His grudging praise has seemed more perceptive
and therefore less quotable than the dismissals of Dr. Johnson
('Nothing odd will do long—*Tristram Shandy* did not last') and
Dr. Leavis ('Sterne's irresponsible (and nasty) trifling'). But
the two latter judgements, separated by two centuries, have
become attached to *Tristram Shandy*, despite the patient
demonstrations of Sterne critics and scholars. The charges
against Sterne, that his most important book is formless and his
jokes indecent, are not easily dismissed. It is not the purpose of
this book to defend him against the objections of Dr. Johnson or
Dr. Leavis, except by putting him in context. A far more
intelligent, alert and appreciative understanding of Sterne the
artist is now becoming evident. The significance of a work of art,
however, is not often triumphantly established in an age
succeeding its composition, though its popularity may wax and
wane. Dr. Johnson was magnificently right when he said in his
Preface to Shakespeare (1765) '. . . no other test can be applied
than length of duration and continuance of esteem.' *Tristram
Shandy* has lasted despite the very oddity which bothered
him—indeed, largely because of it.

Tristram Shandy is its own running commentary. Like Swift's
A Tale of a Tub (and, in a different way, Blake's *The Book of
Urizen*) it is in itself an integral reflexively analytical formal
statement on 'the book' as self-defining, self-limiting yet
unstable, because profoundly ambiguous, artefact. Unless one
brings certain conventional expectations to reading it, a *gestalt*
of what a novel ought to be and usually is, one is not going to
enjoy the joke of having those expectations constantly played

7

with, frustrated, and yet, in the event, partially satisfied after all. *Tristram Shandy* is largely about the imperfections, the radical instability, of words. Sterne refuses to give us an immediately intelligible narrative message, offering instead a practical demonstration of the difficulties of communication, on two levels: communication among the residents of Shandy Hall and its environs, which is blocked or disastrously incomplete; and the writer's communication with us, the readers.

Whether or not Dr. Leavis (or even Dr. Johnson) is to blame, many otherwise cultivated people consider *Tristram Shandy* 'the most boring book ever written'. This description was offered me gratuitously when I chaired the Sterne session at the Canadian Society for Eighteenth-Century Studies annual meeting in 1983. It has been echoed by others, including a Professor of Education in England who, before he left literature to earn his living in another faculty, was a specialist in eighteenth-century satire. To those who find Tristram Shandy boring, one is tempted to say, *Viva la joia, fidon la tristessa!* The in-built residual puritanism of Anglo-American culture is, probably, responsible for the resolute myopia of some critics when they have turned to Sterne. I should make it clear that I do not use the word 'puritan' as a term of abuse, but as culturally descriptive; indeed, there is much in the puritan tradition I find admirable.

The plot of *Tristram Shandy*, fluid and anarchic, is frequently enlisted on the side of modernism. Sterne, in the *persona* of Tristram and in his *Sermons*, broods on riddles, mysteries, body-soul dualism and interaction, and the inconsistencies of human nature. In Sermon XI, 'Evil Speaking', he writes:

> . . . the bulk of mankind live in such a contradiction to themselves, that there is no character so hard to be met with as one, which, upon a critical examination, will appear altogether uniform, and in every point consistent with itself.

This emphasis on instability has led some critics to see *Tristram Shandy* as experimental to the point of rootlessness, a new beginning. Yet, like Fielding, Sterne makes constant structural, as well as allusive, use of Cervantes. Less frequently noted is the old-fashioned rigid psychology of the characterization in

Tristram Shandy; the Shandy brothers both exemplify the 'ruling passion' schema, in its turn the heir of classification by 'humour'. Despite their charm and vitality, Walter and Uncle Toby are each variations on a single theme, monomaniacs: even, in the convenient terminology of E. M. Forster, 'flat' rather than 'rounded' characters. The predictability of Walter's intellectualism, of Uncle Toby's old-soldier decency and simplicity, are still points round which the 'digressive and progressive' work revolves. They live quietly in the country in the opening years of the eighteenth century, one retired from commerce, the other invalided out of the wars, old-fashioned even for their own day. To see Sterne as forerunner of James Joyce is less useful than to consider his work in relation to the dissolution of Augustan values into relativism and subjectivity in the wake of Locke. We can rarely be certain when Sterne is writing with a straight face; we may justifiably ask whether he ever is. It may help us to follow him better, though, if we can manage to spot when he is quoting and expecting us to recognize both the original quotation and the wicked use he makes of it. The task of responding to allusion demands alertness and a wide background of reference in a writer's contemporary readership; it grows harder with every year that passes, as Sterne's culture recedes. The reader who knows something of eighteenth-century sermons (and Sterne's can be read with pleasure still, displaying nimble wits and imaginative insights, as he handles familiar parables like The Good Samaritan and The Prodigal Son and brings them to vivid life), who is familiar with Rabelais and Cervantes and Robert Burton, who has a nodding acquaintance with Hartley, the vibrations and the animal spirits, is thereby better equipped to decide for himself what Sterne is saying, or pretending to say, or deliberately, Madam, *not* saying. . . .

The notorious ambiguity of the book makes it a candidate for fashionable critical approaches. Modernist critiques, though, however seductive, are arguably limiting when applied to the art of the past. One may concede that writing is 'an orphan' as Derrida provocatively puts it, without assuming we are at liberty to import anachronistic interpretations, perverse, because ignorant, misreadings. Books are written by hands of 'skin, hair, fat, flesh, veins, arteries, ligaments, nerves, cartileges, bones', that mortal clay of whose vulnerability and short lease the frail Sterne was constantly aware, as novelist and as clergyman. To read him as if his works were written yesterday, instead of more than two centuries ago, is irresponsibly to misread him. To find the centre of his lived humanity, we must acknowledge that he is not our contemporary; he lived among our grandfathers.

It behoves an editor to declare her bias. My special interest lies in interpretation, the rediscovery of meanings in the light of what used to be called background studies (though the term has given way to the more modish 'perspectives'). I am an unrepentant British empiricist, hoping to build by rule of thumb squarely in the Anglo-American tradition of historical scholarship, as a means towards that historical sympathy which alone can teach us about ourselves. Theoretical system-building seems to me sterile, and the philosophy of language appears marginally relevant to the task of coming to a larger and deeper understanding of works of eighteenth-century literary art. If, since the decay of neo-classicism, the British have been wary of critical theory, it has been from well-founded post-Romantic anxiety about the dangers of substituting analytical formulae for human understanding, mechanical abstraction for sensitive response.

My hope is that the reader will use this book and its apparatus as a guide for his own explorations into the past. It does not aim to provide instant opinion, but a tool for further inquiry. We have worked to offer information and to express ourselves concisely and clearly. We hope to challenge scholars to fresh thought and at the same time offer the beginner a 'way in' to Sterne studies.

Planning this book, I was fortunate in finding contributors willing to tackle issues which, it seemed to me, had attracted too little attention: Sterne's equivocal status as the cleric who published a book full of jokes which Coleridge thought 'scarce readable by women'; the background of eighteenth-century medical thought, not merely as allusion, but a principle in the book's metaphysic; Sterne's 'plagiarisms'. The first two essays deal, in different ways, with the ribaldry: Professor Melvyn New discusses the question of how much explanation is appropriate; Professor Jacques Berthoud finds in the book's

doubles entendres the structural principle which has eluded so
many of its readers. Professors Edward A. Bloom and Lillian
D. Bloom relate Sterne the novelist to Sterne the preacher.
Professor Alan B. Howes traces Sterne's literary descent from
two of his European masters, Rabelais and Cervantes, and
offers a new way of defining their potent influences. Dr. W. G.
Day, who has completed a study of Sterne's borrowings,
agrees with recent critics that, far from innocently following
Locke, Sterne is indulging in mockery; his essay offers fresh
evidence for this viewpoint. Dr. Roy Porter, a medical
historian, writes on Sterne's use of ideas of health, sickness and
'life' itself in the age of Enlightenment, and offers leads into the
relevant history of science. K. G. Simpson sees Sterne as
pre-Romantic (and we do not call it 'heresy' so to do). Looking
backwards from his current work on Jane Austen, Professor
Park Honan interprets her conservatism as a positive reaction
against the Whiggism of Sterne. Dr. Mark Loveridge writes on
Sterne's relation to the Augustan poets. Dr. W. G. Day
contributes a selective bibliography covering the years 1977–
83, supplementing Lodwick Hartley's standard two volumes.
Professor Bruce Stovel, in his essay, '*Tristram Shandy* and the
Art of Gossip', offers a possible reason for Dr. Leavis's
rejection of Sterne.

Towards Dr. Leavis I have a pupil's gratitude, mixed
with considerable exasperation. He habitually declared himself, with pride, to be a 'puritan'. I have not quoted either
Dr. Johnson or Dr. Leavis in order to mock their views in
general. I disagree profoundly with those who argue that
criticism is now challenging the primacy of literature; to adapt
what Hume said about reason and the passions, I believe that
criticism is and ought only to be the slave of literature, and can
never pretend to any other office than to serve and obey it.
Thinking myself a rebel against Leavis's teaching, I absorbed
his hidden curriculum, the importance of historical knowledge.
As an historian before he changed to English, Dr. Leavis took
it for granted that the literary student would 'read round' a
period and know some history. In seminars, it was his practice
to brush aside all considerations except the one that interested
him: 'Is it any good or not?' But for slower wits the ability to
arrive at mature value judgements, like the ability to read

Milton with enjoyment, can only be 'the reward of consummated scholarship'. In his insistence (one-sided though it appeared at the time) that scholarship is, in itself, no substitute for critical penetration, I now recognize wisdom. This collection has been assembled in the sober conviction that scholarship and criticism, far from being enemies, need to be brought, like wit and judgement, into relation, 'to answer one another' (*Tristram Shandy*, Vol. 3, Ch. 20).

Acknowledgements: for generous help of various kinds I wish to thank Professor Arthur Cash, Dr. W. G. Day, Professor Park Honan, Mr. Kenneth Monkman, Professor Melvyn New, Dr. Roy Porter, Professor Arthur Sherbo, Mr. K. G. Simpson and Professor Bruce Stovel.

References: page references to *The Life and Opinions of Tristram Shandy, Gentleman* (in notes, *TS*) are to the Florida edition of Laurence Sterne, ed. Melvyn New and Joan New (Gainsville: University Presses of Florida, 1978); the second page number refers to the World's Classics edition, ed. Ian Campbell Ross (Oxford: Oxford University Press, 1983). Page references to *A Sentimental Journey* (cited as *SJ*) are to Gardner D. Stout's edition (Berkeley: University of California Press, 1967). Sterne's letters, ed. Lewis Perry Curtis (Oxford: Clarendon Press, 1935) are cited as *Letters*. References to the sermons are to the first editions (London, 1760–69); sermons are also identified by title. Locke's *Essay Concerning Human Understanding*, ed. Peter Nidditch (Oxford: Clarendon Press, 1975) is cited as *E.C.H.U.*

Part One:

SEX, LAUGHTER AND DEATH

1

'At the backside of the door of purgatory': A Note on Annotating *Tristram Shandy*

by MELVYN NEW

In Chapter 7 of Volume 7 of *Tristram Shandy*, Tristram enters Boulogne under the suspicious eyes of the residents, several of whom voice various opinions about the traveller's haste:

> 'Tis for high treason, quoth a very little man. . . . Or else for murder; quoth the tall man. . . . No; quoth a third, the gentleman has been committing—— ——.
>   Ah! ma chere fille! said I, as she tripp'd by, from her matins—you look as rosy as the morning. . . . No; it can't be that, quoth a fourth. . . . (p. 585/p. 391)

The last line is, I am certain, the punchline of a joke, although most readers I ask to explicate the passage quite fail to see the joke that is so clear to me. It is often that way with 'jokes', and often that way with *Tristram Shandy*: some will 'get' the joke; others will not 'get' it; and still others, of course, will think they understand when in reality they do not.

For the last ten years I have been editing *Tristram Shandy*, and no problem in the entire project was more difficult than that of determining an annotative strategy for Sterne's jokes. In the past, the dimensions of the problem might have been

15

defined, as Tristram writes, somewhere between 'the *extreams* of DELICACY, and the *beginnings* of CONCUPISCENCE' (Vol. 5, Ch. 1, p. 415/p. 279); James A. Work's fine textbook edition of *Tristram* (1940) and Gardner D. Stout's thorough edition of *A Sentimental Journey* (1967), for example, both demonstrate some reluctance to follow the possibilities of Sterne's humour from motives that do seem to have something to do with delicacy. But it was not delicacy that prevented us from annotating the passage from Chapter 7. Rather, one looks toward the rule of writing Tristram attributes, humorously, to the sixteenth-century Archbishop of Benevento, Giovanni della Casa, 'that the life of a writer . . . [depends] not half so much upon the degrees of his WIT—as his RESISTANCE' (Vol. 5, Ch. 16, p. 447/p. 300). Nothing, it is often said, spoils a joke more than having to explain it; when one is annotating, the temptation is ever present to spoil punchlines by explaining them. Where to start and where to stop was the challenge we faced in annotating *Tristram Shandy*—and in facing it we found ourselves playing the very game Sterne had designed for his readers, a game of sexual discovering, recovering, uncovering. For a work that begins with Tristram's moment of conception (under the covers) and ends with Toby's misconception (the Widow Wadman discovered), it might well be the essential game.

Let us return to the passage in Chapter 7. The punchline I referred to is 'No; it can't be that.' Can't be what? Obviously, it cannot be whatever was the guess of the third gossip, that the 'gentleman has been committing—— ——'. As throughout *Tristram Shandy* the dash here is the imagination's playground, but, as is also true throughout, Sterne carefully orchestrates our play. For some reason, Tristram's courtly tribute to the young woman renders the guess wrong; my conviction is that the guess was 'unnatural acts', that is, a suspicion of homosexual activity, an accusation to which Tristram's courtliness to the young woman supposedly gives the lie. As with so many jokes, this one depends upon a stereotype we might want to dispute, but the humour is nonetheless attempted—and is successful for those who accept, even momentarily, its logic: homosexuals are not interested in women; this stranger shows an interest in women; this stranger cannot be a homosexual.

To annotate this passage with such an explanation is to play out Sterne's game of sexual discovery without giving the reader, if I may so phrase it, a turn at bat. The potential not to uncover the joke at all, or to discover it for oneself, or to find a quite different joke—all options are inherent in the activity Sterne promotes through the conscious sexual potentialities of his language. And insofar as Sterne's game exists at the subconscious as well as conscious level of language use, and exists whether the subject is sex or anything else, to deny the player full participation is to curtail seriously the experience of *Tristram Shandy*.[1]

Is there, then, nothing for the annotator to do with Sterne's game of sexual discovery? Is all such mediation an un-warrantable intrusion between the reader and the text, most especially so when the reader's capacity to 'get' the text is the game being played? Sterne confronts the problem in the first volume of *Tristram*, when he sends madam back to re-read a chapter, punishment for having missed a clue concerning intrauterine baptism. Here the author plays his own annotator or mediator, forcing all his readers to 'get' a text I am certain all will miss on first reading. Clearly, most readers will not have read the 'Memoir of the Doctors of the Sorbonne' *before* reading this passage, and hence the statement 'it was not necessary I should be born before I was christened' (Vol. 1, Ch. 19, p. 64/p. 47) does not bring the *petite canulle* to mind. Sterne's humour depends on requiring from his readers a knowledge they could not possibly be expected to have—as well as on the unexpected stroke of the author's changing his rôle to that of mediator. But the passage does suggest to us one area of annotation that seems legitimate *vis-à-vis* Sterne's sexual humour. Several examples would be useful.

When Tristram arrives in Montreuil (Vol. 7, Ch. 9) he is immediately attracted to the innkeeper's daughter and decides to paint her 'in all her proportions, and with as determined a pencil, as if I had her in the wettest drapery' (p. 589/p. 393). It is perhaps not necessary, in this era of wet T-shirt contests, to explain what Tristram has in mind, and yet it does add to our pleasure, I think, to know two additional facts upon which Sterne's humour is based: (1), as many readers will already know, artists did use wet drapery on models; and (2), as probably few readers will know, the practice was considered appropriate for sculptors but *not for painters*:

> The ancient Statuaries, made their Draperies of wet Linen, on purpose to make them sit close and streight to the Parts of their Figures. . . . Those great Genius's of Antiquity, finding that it was impossible to imitate with Marble the Fineness of Stuffs or Garments . . . thought they could not do better . . . than to make use of such Draperies, as hinder'd not from seeing through their folds, the Delicacy of the Flesh, and the Purity of the Out-lines . . . But Painters, on the contrary, who are to deceive the Sight, quite otherwise than Statuaries, are bound to imitate the different Sorts of Garments, such as they naturally seem. . . .[2]

Sterne had more than a passing interest in painting,[3] and thus was assuredly aware that Tristram's 'wettest drapery' was not legitimate; but until a sufficient context is supplied, most readers would remain somewhat misfocused, vague, in their grasp of the passage.

A second example can be offered, this from the story of the abbess of Andoüillets. On the one hand, the most basic mediation of all, that of translation, is required: the reader lacking French misses the humour lodged in Andoüillets (little sausages, with a bawdy tradition at least as old as Rabelais), and even more obviously, the real 'sinfulness' of *bouger* (to move, with an allusion to *bougre*, bugger) and *fouter* (to fuck), upon which Sterne's joke depends. But what are we to think of the novice with the 'whitloe in her middle finger', brought about by 'sticking it constantly into the abbess's cast poultices, &c.' (Vol. 7, Ch. 21, p. 607/p. 404)? Any reader who has travelled this far into *Tristram Shandy* is bound to be wary of anything finger-shaped being stuck into anything of any shape.[4] That suspicion can be rendered far more certain by knowing something about *et cetera*. Sterne, for example, writes in his *Journal to Eliza*: 'O my dear Lady, cried I, did you but know the Original—but what is she to you, Tristram— nothing; but that I am in Love with her—et ceetera——said She—no I have given over dashes—replied I. . . .'[5] But even more obvious, perhaps, is Fielding in *Shamela*. Parson Tickle-text writes to Parson Oliver about the book: ' "It has stretched out this diminutive mere Grain of Mustard-seed (a poor Girl's little, *&c.*) . . ." ' and Oliver responds, 'naked in Bed, with his Hand on her Breasts, *&c.* . . .'[6] If any doubt remains, we might also turn to the *Oxford English Dictionary*, s.v. *et cetera*, 2.b.: 'as substitute for a suppressed substantive, generally a coarse or indelicate one'.

Similarly, a few pages after this, Sterne plays on the 'whitloe' (an inflammation or swelling), by having the muleteer refer to the novice's having 'got a white swelling by her devotions'. The *O.E.D.* (s.v. *swelling*) indicates this is simply a swelling without redness; Francis Grose, however, in the *Classical Dictionary of the Vulgar Tongue* (1785), offers another usage from the eighteenth century: 'a woman with child is said to have a white swelling.' These instances suggest the ways in which materials could and should be made available to readers of *Tristram Shandy*, without interfering with their reading of the work, and indicate as well some further boundaries for the game of sexual discovery. Every *et cetera* in *Tristram*, or any eighteenth-century book for that matter, does not have a similar connotation; the game remains intact for the reader, made possible, however, by the recovery of a sexual possibility. For example, an earlier passage might need to be reconsidered: 'How do the slight touches of the chisel, the pencil, the pen, the fiddle-stick, *et cætera,*—give the true swell, which gives the true pleasure!' (Vol. 2, Ch. 6, p. 115–16/ p. 81). An awareness of the potentiality of *et cetera* moves backwards to colour 'fiddle-stick', which in turn may have already moved forward to colour '*et cætera*'—and hand in glove, so to speak, both go forward to influence 'swell' and 'pleasure'. It is no accident that Sterne ends this passage with a warning: 'O my countrymen!' [Is there a pun in *country*, again typical throughout the eighteenth century?] '—be nice;— be cautious in your language;——and never, O! never let it be forgotten upon what small particles your eloquence and your fame depend.'

But even more interesting, I think, is the play with 'white swelling'. That one needs to define 'white swelling' is one thing; that the novice's whitloe on her finger, got by sticking it into the abbess's *et cetera*, has somehow become a pregnancy is quite another. Is Sterne sniggering in his usage of 'white

19

swelling' simply for the sake of doing so—using a bawdy expression apropos of nothing except the slight, forbidden pleasure of writing and reading sexual *doubles entendres?*[7] Or is he rather trapping us into perceiving a *double entendre*, which he then withdraws from us? It is logically incoherent for 'white swelling' to mean pregnancy in this context, the contributing elements being so obviously wrong. Have we discovered more than Sterne intended; or did Sterne want us to uncover more than we could logically, reasonably deal with? These are the questions of Sterne's game of sexual discovery, and the annotator should not answer them; but by providing an available meaning of 'white swelling' he has made the game possible.

One more illustration will be useful, this from the end of Volume 7, where Tristram joins the peasant dance:

> They are running at the ring of pleasure, said I, giving him a prick——By saint Boogar, and all the saints at the backside of the door of purgatory, said he . . . I'll not go a step further. . . .
> (Vol. 7, Ch. 43, p. 649/p. 430–31)

The 'ring of pleasure' recurs in *A Sentimental Journey* in a quite similar passage:

> I walked up gravely to the window in my dusty black coat, and looking through the glass saw all the world in yellow, blue, and green, running at the ring of pleasure.—The old with broken lances, and in helmets which had lost their vizards—the young in armour bright. . . .[8]

Stout's note, after accounting for the chivalric exercise of 'running at the ring', makes clear the bawdy meaning available to Sterne, citing Rabelais's delightful retelling of the story of Hans Carvel's 'ring' (III, 28) and the following:

> Some other puffes did swell in length by the member, which they call the labourer of nature, in such sort, that it grew marvellous long, plump, jolly, lusty, stirring, and crest-ridden in the antique fashion . . . : but if it happened the aforesaid member to be in good case . . . then to have seen those strouting champions, you would have taken them for men that had their lances settled on their rest, to run at the ring, or tilting quintain.[9]

St. Boogar takes us back to *bougre*, and as Frank Brady has suggested, this saint presides over a number of events and allusions in *Tristram Shandy*[10]; here the 'pricks' at the 'backside' of the door of purgatory makes the allusion about as clear as one might wish.

But it is the contrast between this cluster of allusions and the dominant image of the chapter, the 'cursed slit' in Nannette's petticoat, that is most arresting. The journey of Volume 7 has seemed to carry us from severe illness to relative restoration, from night-time journeys to the 'sun-burnt daughter of Labour', from neck- and carriage-breaking speed to the natural grace of the country dance. In sexual terms, it has moved from isolation and impotence (most explicitly, the admission of failure with Jenny in Chapter 29) to the invitation of Nannette and the slit in her petticoat. It is a movement Sterne would seem to repeat in *A Sentimental Journey*, which opens with Yorick in his appropriately named *désobligeant*, a one-person carriage[11]; which passes through the episode quoted earlier in which, from his Paris window, Yorick feels his isolation from the world of love and colour below; and which concludes with his hand reaching across the empty space toward the Fille de Chambre's appropriate aposiopesis, but only after the penultimate episode of 'The Grace', the peasant dance so similar to Tristram's encounter with Nannette.

The moment Nannette dances up 'insiduous', Tristram 'dances off', the 'slit' is a 'cursed slit', and Tristram would give 'a crown to have it sew'd up' (Vol. 7, Ch. 43, p. 650–51/ p. 431). Yorick finds '*Religion* mixing in the dance'[12] but nevertheless also dances away and ends, as he began, seeking rather than finding. The road to fulfilment (sexual or otherwise) in *Tristram Shandy* and *A Sentimental Journey* is mined with the complications of language and desire. Like Toby, Tristram may not be able to tell the right end of a woman from the wrong, nor, perhaps, a woman from a man. Like Tristram, Yorick surrenders grace for quest, and *delicacy* and *concupiscence* finally do hold a 'chapter together'—'The Case of Delicacy'—in the very last chapter Sterne was to write. It is not, however, the annotator's rôle to define what the reader might discover in these several plots, but rather to position the reader on the brink of interpretation, to tease that natural and persistent urge to understand the text we confront. In this regard, Sterne shares more with his annotators than with his readers, for his writing seems desperate to avoid fulfilment (completeness) which, it would appear, in the writing of Shandean books is tantamount to defeat. There must always be more to write than days to write it in, more to imply than words can contain, more to imagine than judgement can control. Like Tristram, like Yorick, like Sterne himself, then, the annotator avoids the grace of interpretation and remains on station at the 'backside of the door of purgatory', paying dearly for the possibilities of language and human sexuality, the discoveries already made and the discoveries yet to be made. For the fact is that, however innocent we might be, as innocent indeed as a young novice, a *white swelling* is still pregnant with possibilities. To know that about Sterne's game of sexual discovery is the beginning of wisdom; the end is nowhere in sight, and properly so.

NOTES

1. See Robert Alter, '*Tristram Shandy* and the Game of Love', *American Scholar* 37 (1968), 316–23.
2. C. A. Du Fresnoy, *The Art of Painting*, trans. John Dryden (London, 1716), pp. 142–43. The point is made in other eighteenth-century treatises on painting.
3. See R. F. Brissenden, 'Sterne and Painting', in *Of Books and Humankind: Essays and Poems Presented to Bonamy Dobrée*, ed. John Butt (London: Routledge and Kegan Paul, 1964), pp. 93–108; and William Holtz, *Image and Immortality: A Study of 'Tristram Shandy'* (Providence, R. I.: Brown University Press, 1970).
4. Cf. Robert Gorham Davis, 'Sterne and the Delineation of the Modern Novel', in *The Winged Skull: Papers from the Laurence Sterne Bicentenary Conference* (Kent, Ohio: Kent State University Press, 1971), p. 35: 'Sterne, however, is as insistent as the most orthodox Freudian on the fact that for some imaginations at some times every straight object, every stick, candle, wick, nose can stand for the male genital, and every hole, slit, crevice and curve, for the female.'
5. *Letters*, p. 379.
6. *An Apology for the Life of Mrs. Shamela Andrews*, ed. Sheridan W. Baker, Jr. (Berkeley: University of California Press, 1953), pp. 11, 16; see also p. 75.
7. Recall how Tristram introduces the story: 'My ink burns my finger to try . . .' (Vol. 7, Ch. 20, p. 605/p. 404).
8. *SJ*, pp. 155–56. Stout fails to note that *armour* was an eighteenth-century term for condom, and that 'helmets which had lost their vizards' is almost certainly an allusion to the damage wrought to noses by the treatment with mercury of venereal disease.

A Note on Annotating 'Tristram Shandy'

9. *The Works of Francis Rabelais, M.D.*, trans. Thomas Urquhart and Peter Motteux, with notes by John Ozell, 5 vols. (London 1750), Bk. 2, Chs. 9–10.

10. Frank Brady, '*Tristram Shandy*: Sexuality, Morality and Sensibility', *E.C.S.* 4 (1970), 41–56.

11. *SJ*, p. 76; it is Sterne who identifies it as such in a footnote: 'A chaise, so called in France, from its holding but one person'.

12. Ibid., p. 284.

2

Shandeism and Sexuality

by JACQUES BERTHOUD

1

Book 5 of *Tristram Shandy* opens with an anecdote which proves
that a word may be ruined as easily as a virgin. All you have to
do, it seems, is to pay the wrong sort of attention to it. A lady
of the court of Navarre ominously named La Fosseuse utters
the word 'whiskers' in the hearing of the Queen. She repeats it,
making a curtsey as she does so. Her voice is soft, yet so
articulate that every letter falls distinctly on the Queen's ear.
'There's not a cavalier in Navarre that has so gallant a pair—'
'—Of what?' asks the Queen, smiling. 'Of whiskers', replies
La Fosseuse, *with infinite modesty*. This last stroke is decisive, for
too much innocence is at least as suspicious as too little. The
word is shaken, but it holds its ground. However La Fosseuse
persists in pronouncing it, as she does at every opportunity,
with an accent fraught with 'mystery'. It begins to be
discredited; in the course of half a season's conversation it
becomes indecent; and after a final effort on its part it is
absolutely unfit for use (Vol. 5, Ch. 1, p. 414/p. 279).
    Sterne the moralist tries to suggest that the manners of the
court of Navarre are to blame, declaring that nothing is safe in
a society that combines the extremes of delicacy with the
beginnings of concupiscence. But this is disingenuous. When
he laments that bolsters, night-caps, chamber-pots, placket-
holes, pump-handles and spigots now stand 'on the brink of
destruction', he has already succeeded in pushing them over

24

the brink. The function of his anecdote is less to condemn social prurience than to provoke it. His example is not Mrs. Grundy but La Fosseuse herself; what her infinite modesty does to Navarre, his infinite regard for our virtue does to us. As a result, few of the English nouns that are privileged to appear on the pages of his book remain intact. Ordinary domestic objects like button-holes and candles and empty bottles and sausages and old hats and sealing-wax and slippers and buttered buns start to look like articles in a sex-shop catalogue. Blameless locutions like 'rise up trumps' or 'get it out of him' or 'to make ends meet' turn into ideas we can scarcely permit ourselves to entertain. The infection even spreads to the remoter regions of the language. Uncle Toby's man-servant, Trim, decides one night to show the maid Bridget his master's model fortifications. As they are about to enter the garden arm-in-arm, his *leg* or *peg* or *pin* slips into the *ditch* or *fossé* or *cuvette*; he falls forwards, she falls backwards, and they break the little *bridge*. With the literal-mindedness of the true innocent, Toby's only concern is for the damage to his servant: 'It was a thousand to one . . . that the poor fellow did not break his leg.' But his brother Walter is otherwise entertained: 'Ay truly! . . . a limb is soon broke, brother *Toby*, in these encounters.' And, before we can take in this thrust, the entire siege vocabulary of antiquity has been pressed into new service. The *vinea* of Alexander, the *catapultae* of the Syrians, which cast stones, the *ballista*, the *pyraboli* which cast fire, the *terebra* and *scorpio* which cast javelins: 'But what are these . . .', asks Walter sarcastically, 'to the destructive machinery of Corporal *Trim?*' (Vol. 3, Ch. 24, p. 249/p. 167). There are no defences against the variety and profusion of Sterne's manoeuvres. He even succeeds in making a doctrinal tract suspect—on the grounds that such writings are so empty of meaning that nature, which abhors a vacuum, cannot but insinuate a few improprieties into their readers' vacant heads.

The destabilizing of the common noun in *Tristram Shandy* is so persistent that one might be excused for regarding it as obsessive, if not pathological.[1] Certainly Sterne knows that the reader may take offence, and prepares the standard excuse. Tristram and his friend Eugenius are discussing the possibility of a *double entendre* in the text of the novel.

Here are two senses, cried *Eugenius*, as we walk'd along, pointing with the fore finger of his right hand to the word *Crevice*, in the fifty-second page of the second volume of this book of books,—here are two senses—quoth he—And here are two roads, replied I, turning short upon him—a dirty and a clean one—which shall we take? (Vol. 3, Ch. 31, p. 258/ p.173)

So what dirties a text is how we decide to see it, nor can an author be held responsible for the private smuttiness of his readers. But how seriously are we to take this? The exchange conceals a private joke: Eugenius, here on the side of public decency, is a portrait of John Hall-Stevenson, a notorious rake and pornographer. But we do not have to know this to sense the speciousness of Sterne's retraction. It is so patently glib that it prolongs the affront. Indeed, it has more than a touch of the covert malice which he reserves for authoritarian moralists and critics whenever they appear in the pages of his novel.

Sterne, of course, could have adopted another line of defence. Instead of toying with the rules of propriety, he could have openly confessed that his *doubles entendres* were erotic in intention as well as in effect. Rather than pretend to a virtue he did not believe in, he could have come clean and boldly declared that sex is sex. As a theologian, if in no other capacity, he knew very well that perfectly innocent sex is impossible; to denounce the hypocrisy of purity would have been more genuinely respectable than to indulge his prurient charades. Thus he could have become a forerunner of a great modern movement—the sexual evangelism which, under the slogan *coito ergo sum*, preaches the destruction of sanctimonious order and puritanical power. He would prophetically have aligned himself with contemporary ethics, as his manipulation of narrative illusion has aligned him with modernist criticism.

I shall attempt to demonstrate why he did not take this alternative.

2

When truth 'has slipped us', Tristram says, 'if a man will but take me by the hand, and go quietly and search for it, as for a thing we have both lost, and can neither of us do well without,—I'll go to the world's end with him' (Vol. 5, Ch. 11, p. 439/p. 294). Strasburg will be far enough for our present purpose, whither we must pursue the most elaborate of Tristram's *doubles entendres*. Every reader of the novel will recall that Tristram's father, who is obsessed with noses ('I declare, by that word I mean a Nose, and nothing more, or less') (Vol. 3, Ch. 31, p. 258/p. 174), owns a great library on the subject. Its prize volume, in Latin, by the German scholar and pedant Hafen Slawkenbergius (some think this name means Chamber-pot Slagheap) contains a tale which Tristram translates as a prelude to Book 4 (pp. 288–324/pp. 196–217). In it a courteous stranger, equipped with an enormous nose, one evening unobtrusively enters the city. He is seen by half-a-dozen citizens, but he keeps to himself, and the following morning makes a quiet departure, planning to return in a month. But this passage through the capital of Alsace produces a devastating effect. The city explodes into a frenzy of curiosity and speculation. It divides into two factions, the *nosarians* who believe the nose to be real, and the *antinosarians* who don't. The ordinary people, pragmatic as always, concern themselves with facts: whether the nose bled, whether it was made of wood, or whether it had a pimple; the intellectuals, as is their wont, reason: the college of physicians, the philosophers, the clergy, both the Catholic and the Protestant universities urgently practise 'dialectical induction'. As the date of the stranger's return approaches, the excitement rises to a riot, and the population empties the city to meet him. Meanwhile he has been overtaken by a traveller who identifies him as one Diego, and gives him a letter from his betrothed Julia. We discover that Diego has been driven into mortified exile by her lack of faith in the authenticity of his nose, and that regretting her apostasy she has followed him from Valladolid, only to collapse at Lyons. Diego decides to return to her at once, by-passing the deserted Strasburg—which meantime is silently invested by the French and absorbed into metropolitan France.

The preposterousness of this narrative (which I take to be about the maladjustment of effects and causes) is essential to its point. The huge excitement of the Strasburgians, like the historical fate of their city, is generated by an absurdly insignificant cause—indeed, a cause the reality of which is itself in doubt. The centre of the cyclone is nothing more solid than an ambiguity—or, more precisely, two ambiguities; for the first one—whether such a nose can be real or not—draws its piquancy from a second over which it is superimposed—whether the word has a sexual referent or not. The collective hysteria is fomented by a suspicion—not an affirmation or a denial—transferred, as it were, from reader to participants, that an impropriety may be involved. The tale takes to an extreme a tendency, long recognized as characteristic of the novel as a whole, to defer or abort the narrative point. A city is inflamed with the expectation of the return of a man who fails to materialize; it is consumed with the desire to know who this stranger is, what his business is (he says he comes from 'the Promontory of Noses' and is on his way to 'Crim Tartary'— the very giving famishes the craving), whether his appendage is touchable: they learn *nothing*. The very letter Julia sends Diego ends in a sort of *coitus interruptus*: 'haste as you will—you will arrive but to see me expire.—'Tis a bitter draught, *Diego*, but oh! 'tis embittered still more by dying un—.' Tristram's explanatory note typically only makes things worse: 'Slawken-bergius supposes the word intended was "unconvinced".' Made frantic by this baited missive, Diego, as he waits for his mule to be saddled, starts to scrawl an ode with a piece of charcoal (Tristram says that 'he eased his mind against a wall'!), and interrupts it on an even more ambiguously obscene cry (the ode, p. 322/p. 216). In short, everything about this tale obliges us to find postponement, deferral, absence at the centre of excitement, activity, energy.

It seems to me that the major reason why Sterne cannot be recruited by a modern libertarian ethic is that for him the prohibition that sexuality encounters has been internalized. For Herbert Marcuse, who inspired a revolutionary crusade, sexual life was like an oppressed people, held down by a power external to itself.[2] But this is a naïve view. More recently, Jacques Lacan has argued that prohibition is not external to desire, but part of its essence.[3] Desire springs from what it lacks as it is consumed by what it gains. Secrecy, refusal, absence, therefore, are not antithetical to it, but constitutive of it. To put the point baldly: take away the notion of the forbidden from sex and you take away what makes it sex. This is not to say that the puritanical pornographer is alone capable of true sexual expression; but it may be to suggest that sex as programmed therapy—the regulated release of merely physical tensions—is not a recognizable human experience. In this view, the *real* opponent of desire is the certainty of disclosure, the immobility of possession, the inertia of repletion. Its natural home is the dubiety and suspense of ambiguity. In this respect the *double entendre* must be distinguished from the pun. The pun involves an ambiguity that is fully admitted—signalled by its emitter and recognized by its receiver. The sexual sense of the *double entendre* is suspended between writer and reader: the one can always retain the option of disowning it in favour of the other. It thrives in the twilight of discourse; it requires the tacit and the conspiratorial. It cannot exist in soliloquy, for it depends on collusion. But precisely because neither side can own up, each is more than usually dependent on the other. All reading, of course, is a form of activity, but Sterne's readers are active in a special way: they are forced to become participants.

If we wish to show that Sterne's conception of sexuality is not essentially distasteful (though he is capable of the most deplorable lapses), we can draw attention to its humorousness. But here we come to a difficulty, for, as Walter Shandy puts it, 'there is no passion so serious as lust.' Sexual humour usually works by an effect of distancing and detachment, whereas my argument underlines participation and implication. Sterne affords many examples of sexual humour that works unproblematically through incongruity and surprise:

> But who ever thought, cried *Kysarcius*, of laying with his grandmother?—The young gentleman, replied *Yorick*, whom *Selden* speaks of—who not only thought of it, but justified his intention to his father by the argument drawn from the law of retaliation.—'You lay'd, Sir, with my mother, said the lad—why may not I lay with yours?' (Vol. 4, Ch. 29, p. 393/ p. 264)

The flavour of Yorick's humour is quite different from Tristram's. Its incongruity being of an entirely logical kind, all it requires of its reader is attention to a complete demonstration. Keeping nothing back because it has nothing to conceal it leaves him unimplicated in a situation that is sexual only in name. Tristram's humour, however, requires an entirely different analysis.

3

We may think that Slawkenbergius's tale is now exhausted. ('I know of no tale that could possibly go down after it', says Tristram, quoting his author with malicious naïveté.) But as, having reached the end of the Prologue, we begin Chapter 1, we discover an additional scene: the reconciliation of the lovers in Lyons after their misunderstanding and separation. It is entitled 'The Intricacies of Diego and Julia'.

> Heavens! thou art a strange creature *Slawkenbergius*! what a whimsical view of the involutions of the heart of woman hast thou opened! how this can ever be translated, and yet if this specimen of *Slawkenbergius's* tales, and the exquisitiveness of his moral should please the world—translated shall a couple of volumes be.—Else, how this can ever be translated into good *English*, I have no sort of conception.—There seems in some passages to want a sixth sense to do it rightly.—What can he mean by the lambent pupilability of slow, low, dry chat, five notes below the natural tone,—which you know, madam, is little more than a whisper? The moment I pronounced the words, I could perceive an attempt towards a vibration in the strings, about the region of the heart.—The brain made no acknowledgement.—There's often no good understanding betwixt 'em.—I felt as if I understood it.—I had no ideas.— The movement could not be without cause.—I'm lost. I can make nothing of it,—unless, may it please your worships, the voice, in that case being little more than a whisper, unavoidably forces the eyes to approach not only within six inches of each other—but to look into the pupils—is not that dangerous?— But it can't be avoided—for to look up to the cieling, in that case the two chins unavoidably meet—and to look down into each other's laps, the foreheads come into immediate contact, which at once puts an end to the conference—I mean to the sentimental part of it.—What is left, madam, is not worth stooping for. (Vol. 4, pp. 326–27/pp. 218–19)

This meeting, which is so vividly before us, has no positive existence. It is rendered only through a system of responses.

The *scene* itself cannot be there; it could not literally be there in a piece of fiction, anyway. It is mediated from the original Latin (substantial extracts of which we have seen for ourselves in the Prologue), through Tristram's translation of it ('lambent pupilability'), to Tristram's response to that translation ('I felt as if I understood it'), to Tristram's interpretation of that response ('unless . . . the whisper . . . forces the eyes . . . to look into the pupils'), to Tristram's solicitation of a corroborative response ('your worships . . . madam'). The scene is not so much wrapped up in a succession of narrative layers as evoked, in its absence, by means of a consort of sympathetically vibrating strings. It is as if the renunciation of direct description had driven Sterne to feats of responsive mobility, achieved in collaboration with imagined auditors and real readers.

And what, in turn, of the lovers themselves—the performers of the episode thus evoked? They seem to reproduce with respect to each other the relations established between teller and listener. They are charged with an undeclared reciprocal excitement. They look into each other's eyes; they gaze not at an object but into a returning gaze, in an exchange in which everything is said and nothing is spoken. Their true language takes the form—in Sterne's ostentatiously expressive phrase—of 'lambent pupilability'. In this conversation of glances, sexual feeling is at once offered and held back. It exists as a form of tension, of 'dangerousness', between them, just as the tacit acknowledgement of that tension creates far-from-innocent oscillations of sensibility between Sterne and ourselves.

I have no wish to complicate intolerably these 'intricacies' of Diego and Julia. My main point is plain: that Sterne expresses sexual scenes through innuendo which, because it relies on the knowing reader, draws from him a vivacity eagerly in search of the responses on which it lives. Consider another and more famous gaze: the gaze with which the Widow Wadman at last overcomes Uncle Toby's ten-year indifference to her. She persuades him to look for a grain of sand which she alleges has got into her eye. As long as he does that—that is, as long as he regards the eye as an optical object—he is safe. But let him for a moment realize he is looking at an intentional glance, and he is lost.

I protest, Madam, said my uncle Toby, I can see nothing whatever in your eye.

It is not in the white; said Mrs. Wadman: my uncle Toby look'd with might and main into the pupil—

Now of all the eyes, which ever were created—from your own, Madam, up to those of Venus herself, which certainly were as venereal a pair of eyes as ever stood in a head—there never was an eye of them all, so fitted to rob my uncle Toby of his repose, as the very eye, at which he was looking—it was not, Madam, a rolling eye—a romping or a wanton one—nor was it an eye sparkling—petulant or imperious—of high claims and terrifying exactions, which would have curdled at once that milk of human nature, of which my uncle Toby was made up—but 'twas an eye full of gentle salutations—and soft responses—speaking—not like the trumpet stop of some ill-made organ, in which many an eye I talk to, holds coarse converse—but whispering soft—like the last low accents of an expiring saint—"How can you live comfortless, captain Shandy, and alone, without a bosom to lean your head on—or trust your cares to?"

It was an eye—

But I shall be in love with it myself, if I say another word about it.

—It did my uncle Toby's business. (Vol. 8, Ch. 25, pp. 707–8/p. 466)

We have here, of course, what is perhaps the most extreme example of Sterne's favourite device: the doubling of a character's response (here Toby's) with the writer's and the reader's. This justly celebrated episode exhibits with unusual explicitness Sterne's propensity to be both priest and clerk, reacting directly to his own stimuli, and not only through imagined surrogates. The general effect, obviously, is that we are all equals when it comes to meeting the Widow Wadman's glance. What may be less familiar is the degree to which Sterne's vivacity of inventiveness, which almost turns him into a procurer and ourselves into voyeurs, depends on the *suspected* sexuality of her gaze. It is a gaze that is exactly placed on a scale of implication that includes the knowing innocence of the fashionable lady reading the novel, the venereal power of Venus, the provocative coarseness of an available hussy, and the rococo eroticism of a dying saint. Unambiguous innocence holds no 'converse' at all—like Mrs. Shandy's eye which her husband suddenly encounters as he muses on its potential for 'lewdness':

> Confusion again! he saw a thousand reasons to wipe out the reproach, and as many to reproach himself—a thin, blue, chill, pellucid chrystal with all its humours so at rest, the least mote or speck of desire might have been seen at the bottom of it, had it existed—it did not— (Vol. 8, Ch. 1, p. 736/p. 485).

But the Widow's eye belongs to a woman who can ask herself, within all the tender solicitude she directs at Uncle Toby's wound (now long healed), whether it has impaired his function as a husband. We should note that it is not his fear of impotence that turns off the timid current of his desire, but the discovery beyond all doubt of the real drift of her inquiries. If his wife's unequivocal innocence refrigerates Walter, the Widow's unequivocal lust dispatches Toby into final bachelordom.

4

Sterne's incomparable vivacity, which is the soul of his humour, is founded on his recognition and acceptance of the instability of desire. This he associates with the element of water. Why should a water-drinker (as he oddly asserts) be considered sexually desirable? Tristram seems to believe that 'a rill of cold water dribbling through my inward parts should light up a torch in my Jenny's' (Vol. 8, Ch. 5, p. 660/p. 438). But of course, to hold your being by water is to renounce the ontology of substance.

> —Impetuous fluid! the moment thou presses against the flood-gates of the brain—see how they give way!—
> In swims CURIOSITY, beckoning to her damsels to follow—they dive into the centre of the current—
> FANCY sits musing upon the bank, and with her eyes following the stream, turns straws and bulrushes into masts and bowsprits—And DESIRE, with vest held up to the knee in one hand, snatches at them, as they swim by her, with the other—
> (Vol. 8, Ch. 5, pp. 660–61/p. 438)

In this miniature hedonist's allegory, the self loses its unity in a perpetual play of curiosity, fancy and desire—a *perpetuum mobile* of shifting relations.

The most sustained expression of this motif is the famous Book 7, which takes the form of a lyrical *danse macabre*. Tristram has caught tuberculosis and has been ordered to that sanatorium of nature—Provence. Sterne imagines the journey simultaneously as a headlong flight from a backward menace, Death ('the man with a gun') and as a headlong quest for sanctuary, charmingly evoked as 'that clear climate of fantasy and perspiration'. But this scenario must not be taken too literally. The fear from which he flees is one he carries within him, as is the hope which he pursues.

Sterne's conception of the relationship of death and life is not the least original aspect of his novel. In a study of eighteenth-century medicine, Michel Foucault compares the Renaissance and the Romantic ideas of death; if the Renaissance personifies death as the leveller, laying his icy hand on kings and clowns alike, and if it represents man's mortality as a dance of skeletons celebrating an egalitarian saturnalia, the nineteenth century imagines death as morbidity, as a sort of voluptuousness in which its host discovers his most intimate and secret self—as Foucault suggests, like the funeral card, whose black border isolates and focuses the name inscribed on it.[4] Neither of these is appropriate for Sterne. For him, life and death are too intimately related to accommodate the Renaissance view, too tensely connected to resemble the Romantic view. Tristram's trajectory through France is impelled by quasi-chemical reaction between terror and zest. Its rhythms, from the syncopated hiccups of the Channel crossing to the whip-cracking rattle of the entry into Paris, are musical; they have (in Jean-Jacques Mayoux's vivid phrase) all the verve of a 'heroic scherzo'.[5]

This scherzo is heroic, of course, because it is performed under a spreading darkness. Even at his most carefree, Sterne never loses touch with his inevitable fate. 'So much motion . . . is so much unquietness', says the corpulent Bishop Hall.

> Now, I (being very thin) think differently; and that so much of motion, is so much of life, and so much of joy—and that to stand still . . . is death and the devil—.(Vol. 7, Ch. 13, pp. 592–93/ p. 396)

How sprightly, and yet how sobering, is that three-word parenthesis! In choosing momentum, he does not abolish fixity, any more than a train passenger wishing to feel his speed will ignore the telegraph poles. According to Sterne, we can travel in two ways: with a guide book, looking at monuments, or with our wits awake, watching the inn-keeper's daughter.

> Your worships chuse rather that I give you the length, breadth and perpendicular height of the great parish church . . . but he who measures thee, Janatone, must do it now—thou carriest the principles of change within thy frame; and considering the chances of a transitory life, I would not answer for thee a moment. . . . (Vol. 7, Ch. 9, p. 589/p. 393)

Janatone dwells in the shadow of Montreuil's great church; its rigid perpendiculars are the measure of her transient beauty; if it did not exist Tristram could not 'chuse' her.

Why this should be so, a brief glance at an immense question—Sterne's treatment of time—may make a little clearer. In 'chusing' Janatone, he chooses knowledge of transitoriness. But the passing of time cannot be known directly; like speed, it can only be experienced as a differential relation. At the most general level, the two poles between which this relation oscillates can be identified as nature and art. At one extreme, as individuals born to die, we are helplessly subject to the remorseless chronology of nature. At the other extreme, as beings born to consciousness, we can command this chronology by representing it artistically or ritualistically. These two extremes may seem antithetical, but they rejoin each other in that they prohibit all experience of transitoriness. To be entirely submerged in real time is not to be conscious—to be asleep, or dead, or (if such a thing could be possible) continually present, that is, incapable of the least memory or foresight. To be entirely absorbed in represented time—in story or in dance—is to become oblivious of the chain of temporality, to enter into the freedom of an imagined immortality. God is the maker of real chronology; its laws are His and will not be reversed for us. Man is the inventor of represented chronology; in its space he sheds his helplessness and becomes its god.

Sterne's disruptions of chronology are too well known to require further demonstration here.[6] His capricious expansion of trivial events and contractions of major ones, his malicious indulgence in so-called digressions recklessly scattered over past and future, his mock dismay at being overtaken by the life he is trying to record, etc. have long been recognized as an unmasking of the conventions of literary illusionism. This is indeed so, but it is scarcely adequate for, as A. A. Mendilow has shown,[7] the novel's apparently random incidents are meticulously correlated to a consistent calendar whose major dates are an ostentatiously recollected birth and anticipated death. We would be more faithful to its individual effect if we thought of it as designed to suspend its readers between real and represented time, or nature and art. Its disruptions are not mainly intended to teach us the tedious lesson that literature is mere artifice and writers a trace on it. Their major function is to awaken in us the suspicion (if I may so put it) that the fictive hero may in fact be the author who over hastily dipped his pen in an inkwell as he stifled a chronic cough. Is Tristram Sterne, or was Sterne Tristram? Attentive readers of this paper will quickly discover that I, for one, have found it impossible to decide.

Sterne's commitment to mutability and transience entails a necessary ambiguity of the self. At the climax of his flight through France Tristram finds himself confronted by an importunate official.

> —My good friend, quoth I—as sure as I am I—and you are you—
> —And who are you? said he.—Don't puzzle me; said I.
> (Vol. 7, Ch. 33, p. 633/p. 421)

Why is it that we cannot imagine this riposte ever becoming a slogan of modern deconstruction? It is not that its gaiety would be out of place in the extravagances of post-structural scepticism. It is rather that the ambiguity of the self in Sterne bears no resemblance to the proliferations of that semantic indeterminacy that obsesses contemporary critics. The insouciance and irreverence of his reply (an implicit renunciation of the possibility of unitary definitions) take their impulse from the fact that passports exist. 'Is fickleness taxable in France?' he asks a startled debt-collector (Vol. 7, Ch. 35, p. 638/p. 423); the playfulness relies on the law it mocks. When, therefore, I argue that Sterne's responsiveness to change is dependent on a suppressed chronology (whether real or represented), I am claiming that its suppression is not unlike the suppression of the sexual meaning in a *double entendre*. In fact, the name 'Tristram' could be regarded as the novel's ultimate *double entendre*; just as our suspicion that an impropriety may be in play is sustained by our secret bawdiness, so our suspicion that the mortal Laurence Sterne may lurk behind his fictional hero is nourished by our certainty that the reader is our contingent, temporary self. In this context, desire becomes the novel's inimitable liveliness, and sexuality is turned into Shandeism.

In a volume published in 1982 entitled *Against Criticism* Iain McGilchrist threw out the suggestion that Sterne is a monist, who emphasizes the interdependence of body and soul rather than their opposition.[8] This is, of course, explicit in *Tristram Shandy*'s sprinkling of epigrams on the reciprocity of spirit and sense. It is also articulated in the organization of the novel as a whole, particularly in the parallel it sustains between the brothers Walter and Toby.[9] Referring to Toby's 'amours' which occupy the last two books, Tristram requires us to note the difference between *my father's ass* and *my uncle's hobby-horse*. Walter's ass is his body, which kicks with concupiscent lust and needs curbing. Toby's hobby-horse is a harmless pastime reducing the horrors of war to pacific make-believe. Walter falls into the intellectualist error of heightening the distinction between soul and body. Seeking to dominate life (the conception, birth, nurturing and education of his son) by means of an incorrigibly theoretical programme, he not only registers a succession of failures but completely alienates himself from his own sexuality. Toby, on the other hand, falls into the anti-intellectualist fallacy of obliterating the distinction between soul and body by dissolving both into a conception of life as play. When he falls in love, he does not rage, like his brother, against his subjection; instead, he quietly transforms the 'poison' that seeps through him into domestic and familial sentiment. 'I think when a man is in *love*, it behoves him a little to consider which of the two [brain or liver] he is fallen into', Walter tells him. 'What signifies it', Toby replies, 'which of the two it is, provided it will but make a man marry, and love his wife, and get a few children' (Vol. 8, Ch. 33, p. 718/p. 472).

Laurence Sterne: Riddles and Mysteries

Toby turns his love into a hobby-horse indeed—the one to be found in the nursery.

Because he is prepared to exist between these two extremes, Tristram escapes the fixity of the one and the inertia of the other. His is the monism of ambiguity, neither highlighting the body-soul distinction into antagonism, like his father, nor blurring it into amorphism, like his uncle. To find an emblem for the space he occupies, all we have to do is to recall the intricacies of Diego and Julia. The flame-like language they speak through the eyes—the 'sentimental' part of their discourse, as opposed to mere chat or mere sex—is made possible by the distance that separates them; it is too narrow to make them look directly upwards or directly downwards, towards heaven or towards nature, but it is wide enough to prevent them from ignoring these alternatives.

NOTES

1. See Jean-Jacques Mayoux, 'Laurence Sterne', trans. by John Traugott from 'Laurence Sterne parmi nous', Critique, XVIII, No. 177 (February 1962), 99–120, in Laurence Sterne: Twentieth Century Views, ed. John Traugott (New Jersey: Prentice Hall, 1968), pp. 108–25. This brilliant essay emphasizes Sterne's exhibitionism.
2. I refer, of course, to the use to which One Dimensional Man was put. Marcuse's own position is subtler: see Eros and Civilisation (London: Routledge & Kegan Paul, 1956), 'Epilogue: Critique of Neo-Freudian revisionism'.
3. See, for example, 'L'instance de la lettre dans l'inconscient', Ecrits I (Paris: Editions du Seuil, 1966), 249–89.
4. Michel Foucault, The Birth of the Clinic, trans. A. M. Sheridan from Naissance de la Clinique (Paris: Presses Universitaires de France, 1962; London: Tavistock, 1976), pp. 170–72.
5. Mayoux, p. 123.
6. See, for example, Victor Shklovsky, 'Sterne's Tristram Shandy: Stylistic Commentary' (trans. L. T. Lemon) in Russian Formalist Criticism: Four Essays (Lincoln, Nebraska: University of Nebraska Press, 1965), pp. 25–57.
7. A. A. Mendilow, Time and the Novel (London: Peter Nevill, 1952), pp. 158–59.
8. Iain McGilchrist, Against Criticism (London: Faber, 1982), pp. 131–75.
9. For what follows, see Vol. 8, Chs. 32–4. For an admirable discussion of the philosophical implications of the contrast between Walter and Toby in relation to Locke, see A. D. Nuttall, A Common Sky (London: Sussex University Press, 1974), pp. 45–91.

3

Laurence Sterne, Rabelais and Cervantes: The Two Kinds of Laughter in *Tristram Shandy*

by ALAN B. HOWES

In a letter written a few weeks before his death in 1768 Laurence Sterne complained that it was 'too much to write books and find heads to understand them'. He realized, however, that 'it is not in the power of any one to taste humour . . . 'tis the gift of God—. . . besides, a true feeler always brings half the entertainment along with him.' It is 'like reading *himself* and not the *book*'.[1] Eight years earlier when the first instalment of *Tristram Shandy* had appeared, one reviewer whose enthusiasm was equalled by his bewilderment had written: 'Oh rare Tristram Shandy!—Thou very sensible— humorous — pathetick — humane — unaccountable! — what shall we call thee?—Rabelais, Cervantes, What?'[2]

The 'power of any one to taste humour' may indeed be 'the gift of God', since both Sterne's contemporary readers and those of subsequent generations have often been as baffled, if as enthusiastic, as that early reviewer. Sterne's humour does defy classification, but at the same time, as the reviewer apparently sensed, it is compounded in part from two quite well established traditions, particularly as exemplified in two of Sterne's favourite authors, Rabelais and Cervantes.[3]

François Rabelais published his *Gargantua and Pantagruel* in four instalments between 1532 and 1552. (A fifth instalment of disputed authenticity was published posthumously in 1562.) With folk tales of a race of giants as his starting point, in Books I and II Rabelais begins the exuberant life stories of Gargantua and his son, Pantagruel, including their upbringing and education, and the adventures of Pantagruel and his lifelong friend Panurge. Topics range all the way from how Gargantua 'by a long and curious experience' found that 'of all torcheculs, arsewisps, bum fodders, tail napkins, bung-hole cleansers, and wipe-breeches, there is none in the world comparable to the neck of a goose . . . if you hold her neck betwixt your legs' (I, xiii; Vol. 1, p. 36), to how Gargantua designed the Abbey of Thélème, with the motto 'Do what thou wilt', as an exact opposite to the narrow, stifling, and corrupt monasticism of Rabelais's time. Book III is mainly devoted to Panurge's search for an answer to the question of whether he should marry and to his worries about becoming a cuckold. In Book IV Pantagruel and Panurge set out on a voyage to consult the oracle of the holy bottle, having first filled their ship with the 'wonderful' and 'sacred' herb Pantagruelion, a species of cannabis which they value chiefly as a source for hemp fibres to make rope, but also for its narcotic qualities. They sail by numerous islands, each with its own peculiarities: on one the inhabitants 'have their noses shaped like an ace of clubs' (IV, ix; Vol. 2, p. 123); on another the natives 'live on nothing but wind, eat nothing but wind, and drink nothing but wind' (IV, xliii; Vol. 2, p. 189). In Book V Rabelais (or his successor) completes the account of the quest for the holy bottle after Panurge and Pantagruel have visited other islands.

In *Gargantua and Pantagruel*, Rabelais's humour is primarily what I shall call the *comedy of reference*. This tradition survives today in the stand-up comedian on tour who mentions local spots (often with funny-sounding names or risqué associations), as well as attitudes and subjects (often semi-forbidden) of current or topical interest. The humour derives in part from hearing something mentioned that one might not expect to hear, and may involve the breaking of a taboo. It may also involve play with the sounds of words and their combinations, or with puns or *doubles entendres*. But behind these references there is often a satirical purpose as we perceive a connection between the immediate topic and some common-sense attitude or ideal state which contrasts with it. Thus the double reference may bring together the real world and a fantastic or an ideal world.

Rabelais delineates a fantastic world of giants, but he makes frequent references to real world everyday activities—eating, drinking, sex, and bodily functions. The fact that these subjects, some of them taboo, are talked about, often with exaggeration, creates laughter; and in a preliminary poem addressed to his readers Rabelais states that laughter is his only purpose. But in the Prologue which follows this disclaimer, he warns that there is also a serious satirical dimension to his work, which resembles the Sileni:

> Sileni of old were little boxes . . . painted on the outside with wanton toyish figures . . . to excite people unto laughter . . . ; but within those capricious caskets . . . were carefully preserved and kept many rich and fine drugs . . . with several kinds of precious stones, and other things of great price. . . . Therefore is it, that you must open the book, and seriously consider of the matter treated in it. Then shall you find that it containeth things of far higher value than the box did promise. . . . (The Author's Prologue to Bk. I; Vol. 1, pp. 3–4)

Behind the rollicking voice we at first hear dedicating his book to 'illustrious drinkers, and . . . thrice precious pockified blades' (ibid., p. 3), there is another voice talking of controversial contemporary issues boldly enough to get the book censored.

Rabelais describes Book I on the title page as 'a book full of Pantagruelism', and in Pantagruelism laughter and the serious meet. It is an attitude associated with a boisterous and light-hearted way of life, but it also maintains 'a certain jollity of mind' even when it is 'pickled in the scorn of fortune' (The Author's Prologue to Bk. IV; Vol. 2, p. 95), thus enabling 'good Pantagruelists . . . to live in peace, joy, health', and to be 'always merry'. It is the foe of hypocrites and 'squint-minded fellows' (II, xxxiv; Vol. 1, p. 247). Underlying the laughter, in other words, is a vein of seriousness, and Rabelais sometimes uses the laughter in order to make comments on the religion, the politics, the economics of sixteenth-century France that he could not otherwise make under the censorship that prevailed. Thus the comedy of reference in Rabelais is sometimes simply for the sake of laughter; but often it is a way of attacking indirectly the dying scholasticism of the Middle Ages and espousing the new humanism of the Renaissance with its emphasis on the body, the worldly present rather than the spiritual future, the dignity of the individual and his right to freedom of thought. Starting with folk tales and legends of giants, Rabelais constructs a world with references which echo back and forth with the real world of his time.

Born just five years before the fourth book of *Gargantua and Pantagruel* appeared, Miguel de Cervantes did not publish the first part of his masterpiece, *Don Quixote*, until he was 58; the second part appeared ten years later in 1615, the year before his death. Cervantes's starting-point is the many romances of chivalry that had been published in Spain and other countries, with their accounts of superhuman feats, impossible adventures, and unattainable ideals of conduct. What would happen, he asks himself, if one tried now to live by their chivalric codes? To answer this question, he takes as his hero a country gentleman, Don Quixote, who has become so obsessed with the tales of knight-errantry he reads day and night that his wits have turned and he sallies forth in quest of adventures and opportunities to aid the oppressed, mistaking windmills for giants, inns for castles, a flock of sheep for a human army. Even when he sees things as they are, he believes that powerful enchanters have changed their outward appearance. He is laughed at, taken advantage of, beaten; the code of the knight-errant leads at best to inconvenience, at worst to pain and disaster, in the modern world. Thus, Cervantes tells us in his Preface, his 'superficial Design' is to provide 'Mirth and Humour', but his 'principal End' is 'the Fall and Destruction of that monstrous Heap of ill-contriv'd Romances, which . . . have so strangely infatuated the greater Part of Mankind' (Pt. I, The Author's Preface to the Reader, p. [22]).

Although Cervantes's *Don Quixote* springs initially from the comedy of reference used for satirical purposes, and he points out the implausibilities of many of the stories of knight-errantry which have crazed his protagonist, very soon we see another kind of comedy developing, especially in the relationship between Don Quixote and Sancho Panza, the peasant whom the Don persuades to accompany him as his squire. Sancho is the realist who sees clearly that a windmill is a windmill, an inn is an inn, a flock of sheep is a flock of sheep. But Sancho often gets in as much trouble as his master because of Don Quixote's vagaries. 'I neither am, nor ever mean to be a Knight-Errant,' he tells Don Quixote, 'and yet, of all the Misadventures, the greater Part falls still to my Lot' (I, iii, 3; p. 104). And Sancho's view of the world has its own limitations: he is naïve and uneducated, and often as gullible as his master; he is shrewd without being wise. He agrees to accompany Don Quixote because the Don tells him they are sure to find and conquer an island for Sancho to govern.

Starting with 'The Master's Madness, and the Servant's Simplicity' (I, iv, 3; p. 249), Cervantes builds his comedy from their frustrating difficulties in communicating with each other, and the clashes between the two and the real world of sixteenth-century Spain, both arising inevitably from the ingrained habits and attitudes of master and servant. When Don Quixote admonishes Sancho not to 'overlard your common Discourse with that glut of Proverbs, which you mix in it continually', Sancho replies:

> Alas! Sir . . . this is a Disease that Heaven alone can cure. . . . But henceforwards I'll set a Watch on my Mouth, and let none fly out, but such as shall befit the Gravity of my Place. For in a rich Man's House the Cloth is soon laid; where there's Plenty the Guests can't be empty. A Blot's a Blot till 'tis hit. He's safe who stands under the Bells; You can't eat your Cake and have your Cake; and Store's no Sore.

We can imagine Don Quixote shaking his head in frustration as he points out to Sancho that he has just uttered 'a whole Litany of old Saws, as much to the Purpose as *the Last Year's Snow*' (II, iv, 42, pp. 723–24). This comedy of obsessions, cross purposes and comic clashes is very different from the comedy of reference and I shall call it the *comedy of character*.

The comedy of character is rooted in human limitations and human eccentricities and in the difficulties and frustrations

43

inherent in human beings' attempts to communicate with each other, as well as in the comic distresses of a world in which things often go perversely and not to our liking. This tradition survives in the comic clash of the stand-up comic duo who cannot understand each other because they are talking at cross purposes; in the feeling of frustration of the person who is always slipping on the banana peel that seems to have appeared out of nowhere; in our perceptions of a character's blindness, eccentricity, or narrowness of view, which can range all the way from naïveté or ignorance to obsession or madness.

The comedy of character may also contain satire, focusing on the weakness or blindness of the individual, or on the illogic, hypocrisy or cruelty of the world with which he clashes, or on both. Satire in the comedy of character differs, however, from satire in the comedy of reference. In the satire deriving from reference, the emphasis is on the idea, attitude or social condition represented by the person or thing being satirized, while in the comedy of character the focus is upon the mental processes and feelings of the characters. The comedy of reference is likely to be scattershot with many targets, while the comedy of character is more sustained and is likely to spring from a single trait or source within a character. Our laughter at the comedy of reference is either detached and intellectual, or merely visceral; while our laughter at the comedy of character is sympathetic or empathetic.

In a passage in the second instalment of *Tristram Shandy*, Sterne invokes 'the ashes of my dear *Rabelais*, and dearer *Cervantes*' (Vol. 3, Ch. 19, p. 225/p. 151) and other allusions occur throughout his work. We can trace his lifelong acquaintance with the two writers back to pieces he wrote nearly twenty years before *Tristram Shandy*, when he had a brief fling at politics in an attempt to advance his fortunes as a young clergyman. His letter of 10 November 1741 to the *York Courant* speaks of 'a Disappointment . . . [which] might be allowed a sufficient Cause to exasperate a Don QUIXOT . . .', and in another letter in the same issue he characterizes an opponent through a Rabelaisian comparison with a 'certain nasty Animal in *Egypt*' who 'covers his Retreat with the fumes of his own Filth and Excrement'.[4]

One could not perhaps expect many traces of either Rabelais or Cervantes in the sermons which Sterne was writing then and over the next few years, but in 'Philanthropy Recommended' (Sermon III) he apparently inserted a Rabelaisian joke. He refers to 'the general heads of our duty to GOD and MAN as delivered in the 18th of Leviticus', but this topic is covered in the nineteenth chapter of Leviticus while the eighteenth contains a long catalogue of relatives and others with whom it is unlawful to have sexual intercourse.[5] And if Lansing Hammond's conclusion is correct that 'practically all' of Sterne's sermons were composed before 1751 with only slight alterations when they were later published,[6] then portraits which have some Cervantic humour may well belong to this earlier period. There is Solomon

> . . . whose excess became an insult upon the privileges of mankind; for by the same plan of luxury, which made it necessary to have forty thousand stalls of horses,—he had unfortunately miscalculated his other wants, and so had seven hundred wives, and three hundred concubines.——[7]

And there is the Prodigal Son: 'The apes and the peacocks, which he had sent for from Tharsis, lay dead upon his hands . . .' and 'the mummies had not been dead long enough, which had been brought him out of Egypt; . . . all had gone wrong since the day he forsook his father's house'.[8] The picture of Solomon, overwhelmed by mere 'miscalculation' with an excess of wives and concubines, is indeed humorous, as is that of the frustrated and unlucky Prodigal Son with his dead apes and peacocks and his fake mummies that have not been dead long enough to be genuine. These pictures of comic distress and frustration are typical of the comedy of character.

The comedy of character also demands of both writer and reader a certain nimbleness of perspective in order to achieve another quality which Sterne found in Cervantes. 'I am perswaded,' he writes to a friend who had commented on the manuscript of *Tristram Shandy* in the summer of 1759, 'that the happiness of the Cervantic humour arises from this very thing—of describing silly and trifling Events, with the Circumstantial Pomp of great Ones' (*Letters*, p. 77). Don Quixote's battle against the sheep whom he takes for an army is described as if it were a real battle, his struggle against the windmills is described as if it were a struggle against real giants, and this technique of juxtaposing perspectives enables Cervantes to bring out the humour inherent in the limitations of Don Quixote's view of the world.

Long before *Tristram Shandy*, Sterne had played with a juxtaposition of perspectives in a brief fantasy or meditation, inspired in part by thoughts about the telescope and the microscope, both relatively recent inventions. Falling asleep among his plum trees, he dreams of a cataclysm, but wakes to find there has merely been a windstorm in his orchard. In his reverie he realizes that '*Plumbs* fall, and *Planets* shall perish', and that it is 'hard to say' whether the 'solar system or a drop of pepper water afford[s] a nobler subject of contemplation; in short whether we owe more to ye Telescope or microscope'. Comedy arises when one can't understand the limitations of one's own perspective, when one confuses the world of the telescope with that of the microscope and thinks that plums are as important as planets. Sterne thinks that probably the inhabitants of the 'most inconsiderable Planet that Revolves round ye most inconsiderable Star . . . look upon *their world* . . . as ye only one' and believe that the stars 'were created with ye only view of twinkling upon such of them, as have occasion to follow their cattle late at night'.[9] The comedy of character laughs at those whose view of the world is so narrow and self-enclosed that they believe the stars shine just for them.

The work which directly precedes *Tristram Shandy* shows Sterne beginning to combine the two kinds of comedy. Early in 1759 Sterne had printed but immediately suppressed a little pamphlet entitled *A Political Romance*, as his contribution to a squabble in the York church over the awarding of some ecclesiastical offices. In this satirical 'allegory', as he calls it, Sterne ridicules the participants, reducing the ecclesiastical quarrel to a fight over an old coat. He appends a 'key', which supposedly describes the way his story has been interpreted by different people:

——Thus every Man turn'd the Story to what was swimming uppermost in his own Brain;—so that . . . there were full as

many Satyres spun out of it,—and as great a Variety of
Personages, Opinions, Transactions, and Truths, found to lay
hid under the dark Veil of its Allegory, as ever were discovered
in the thrice-renowned History of . . . *Gargantua* and *Pantagruel*.[10]

Like Rabelais, Sterne has used the comedy of reference for
satirical purposes, and the figures in the 'allegory' stand for
ones in real life. But at the same time, he is beginning to move
toward the comedy of character, for 'every Man turn'd the
Story to what was swimming uppermost in his own Brain'.
The world of *Tristram Shandy*, in which Toby's single-minded
pursuit of his military hobby is matched by Walter's development of his favourite theories with equal tenacity, is already
taking shape, and we are only a step away from the clashes
between characters who have comic difficulties in communicating with each other because each is pursuing what is
'swimming uppermost in his own Brain'.

The step from *A Political Romance* to the first two volumes of
Tristram Shandy is nonetheless a fairly long one and we have
only limited evidence to help us deduce how that step was
taken. In May of 1759 Sterne wrote to London publisher
Robert Dodsley, offering him the manuscript of *Tristram
Shandy*, which he described as 'taking in, not only, the Weak
part of the Sciences, in wch the true point of Ridicule lies—but
every Thing else, which I find Laugh-at-able in my way—'
(*Letters*, p. 74). Dodsley refused the manuscript and Sterne set
about revisions. During the summer he wrote to a friend, who
had read the manuscript and apparently urged Sterne to be
more circumspect in keeping up his clerical character, that he
had not gone 'as farr as Swift', who 'keeps a due distance from
Rabelais' (*Letters*, p. 76). At the same time Sterne would aim
for 'the happiness of the Cervantic humour' (*Letters*, p. 77). By
October he was ready to write to Dodsley and describe the
changes he had made. 'All locality is taken out of the book—
the satire general', he says (*Letters*, p. 81). Apparently Sterne
had been making his book somewhat less Rabelaisian,
somewhat more Cervantic, and had been removing satirical
references to local targets.

This surmise is borne out by another piece of evidence, the
surviving manuscript of a 'Rabelaisian Fragment', which

Melvyn New believes Sterne must have written at this time.[11] A group of Rabelaisian characters is assembled 'keruko-paedizing together', or talking about the art of making sermons. Longinus Rabelaicus, the leader of the group and 'as Rabelaic a Fellow as ever piss'd', introduces a proposal 'with as much Pomp & Parade as he could afford', before being interrupted by Panurge:

> . . . if all the scatter'd Rules of the KERUKOPAEDIA, could be but once carefully collected into one Code, as thick as Panurge's Head, and the whole *cleanly* digested—(Shite! says Panurge, who felt himself aggrieved—). . . .[12]

Meanwhile Homenas, 'who had to preach next Sunday (before God knows whom)', is composing his sermon in the next room, 'Rogering it as hard as He could drive', or plagiarizing from Dr. John Rogers, which allows Sterne to make the pun on 'roger' in the slang meaning of 'copulate'. Although Sterne has cancelled the reference to Rogers and finally substituted one to Dr. Samuel Clarke, thus sacrificing the pun, echoes of the original *double entendre* persist in the sentences which follow:

> having foul'd two clean Sheets of his own, and being quite stuck fast in the Enterance upon his third General Division, & finding Himself unable to get either forwards or backwards—with any Grace——'d--n it,' says He. . . .

Homenas then imagines what will be reported if his plagiarism is found out:

> *Homenas was got upon Dr. Clark's back. . . . He has broke his Neck, and fractured his Skull and beshit himself into the Bargain, by a fall from the Pulpit two Stories high.* Alass poor Homenas!—Homenas has done his Business!

Sterne says (with a triple pun on meanings of 'do one's business': 'do for or ruin', 'ease oneself', and 'copulate'). Homenas concludes, 'I shall never again, be able to tickle it off as I have done', with a final sexual overtone accompanying the primary meaning of 'bring to a satisfactory result'.[13] As is often the case in *Tristram Shandy*, Sterne engages in an extended passage of *double entendre* while pretending to be talking innocently about other matters. The bawdier and more direct references in Rabelais have become subtilized and subordinated to the portrayal of human character and human interactions with the delineation of the self-important Longinus Rabelaicus, the 'aggrieved' Panurge, and the frustrated Homenas.

The characters in the first instalment of *Tristram Shandy* are much more fully developed, but some of them are developed along the same lines as those in his Rabelaisian fragment. There is the self-important Dr. Slop, who wishes to be called '*Accoucheur*' rather than 'man-midwife' (Vol. 2, Ch. 12, p. 130/ p. 90). There is the frustrated Walter Shandy, who is 'baffled and overthrown in all his little systems and wishes' with 'a train of events perpetually falling out against him . . . as if they had purposedly been plann'd and pointed against him, merely to insult his speculations', so that one must believe that some 'malignant spirit took pleasure, or busied itself in traversing the purposes of mortal man' (Vol. 1, Ch. 19, p. 64/ 47). But there is a wider range of characters, again recalling Cervantes. There is Yorick, who is complimented by a comparison with 'the honest refinements of the peerless Knight of *La Mancha*' (whom Sterne loves 'more . . . than the greatest hero of antiquity'), though Yorick is as ill-equipped to deal with the everyday world as Don Quixote was: 'he was utterly unpractised in the world; and, at the age of twenty-six, knew just about as well how to steer his course in it, as a romping, unsuspicious girl of thirteen' (Vol. 1, Ch. 10, p. 23/ p. 19; Ch. 11, p. 27/p. 22). There is Uncle Toby, who has 'almost as many . . . books of military architecture, as Don *Quixote* was found to have of chivalry' (Vol. 2, Ch. 3, p. 102/ p. 73), and who pursues his military hobby as obsessively as Don Quixote pursued knight-errantry.

Each character lives in a limited world, whether it be the 'small circle . . . of four *English* miles diameter' which is the realm in which the midwife has 'no small degree of reputation' (Vol. 1, Ch. 7, p. 10/p. 11); or the miniature world of the homunculus, who is 'as truly our fellow-creature as my Lord Chancellor of England' (Vol. 1, Ch. 2, p. 3/p. 6); or the infuriating (to Walter Shandy) constrictions of Mrs. Shandy's mental sphere:

Cursed luck!——said he to himself . . . for a man to be master of
one of the finest chains of reasoning in nature,——and have a
wife at the same time with such a head-piece, that he cannot
hang up a single inference within side of it, to save his soul from
destruction. (Vol. 2, Ch. 19, p. 172/p. 117)

The limitations of the characters' worlds lead to comic clashes
deriving from two sources. There are the comic frustrations
from the real difficulties in communication—Walter Shandy
can never 'hang up a single inference' inside Mrs. Shandy's
head and he is often at a loss to know what Uncle Toby is
talking about when the latter rides his military hobby-horse.
But there are also comic irritations from perceiving another
character's obsession. Walter is often nettled more by the zeal
and single-mindedness with which Toby and Trim pursue
their hobby than by any difficulties in understanding what
they say. Sterne points to these two sources for the comedy of
character when he speaks of 'the unsteady uses of words which
have perplexed the clearest and most exalted understandings'
(Vol. 2, Ch. 2, p. 100/p. 71), and, in another passage,
describes the nature of obsessions: 'When a man gives himself
up to the government of a ruling passion,—or, in other words,
when his HOBBY-HORSE grows head-strong,—farewell cool
reason and fair discretion!' (Vol. 2, Ch. 5, p. 106/p. 75).

While the mainsprings for characterization thus seem much
closer to Cervantes than to Rabelais, there are nonetheless
evidences of Rabelais throughout the first instalment of
Tristram Shandy. Most obvious are the satire on legal language
and procedure in the midwife's licence and Tristram's
mother's marriage settlement, and the satire on religious
hair-splitting in the Memorandum presented to the Doctors of
the Sorbonne concerning the possibility of baptizing a child in
the mother's womb. There are the *doubles entendres* and sexual
references in the words Sterne invents for kinds of arguments
(*Argumentum Tripodium* or 'argument to the third leg' and
Argumentum ad Rem or 'argument to the thing'), the names he
derives from other languages (Kunastrokius and Coglionissimo,
the latter from the Italian word for 'testicle'), and the sly
suggestion that Trim was thought by the cook and the
chamber-maid to 'know as much of the nature of strong-holds
as my uncle *Toby* himself' (Vol. 2, Ch. 5, p. 109/p. 77).

Sterne also echoes Rabelais's warning that, like the Sileni, his work may be more serious than it at first appears: 'if I . . . should sometimes put on a fool's cap with a bell to it . . . don't fly off,—but rather courteously give me credit for a little more wisdom than appears upon my outside . . .' (Vol. 1, Ch. 6, pp. 9–10/p.10). But there are relatively few 'pure' Rabelaisian passages, and Sterne usually uses the comedy of reference to aid in characterization and in presenting the comic clash of characters. In the very first chapter, for example, Tristram's conception is being described and the underlying references to the context of sexual intercourse are reinforced by the two possible meanings of 'interrupt' brought out by Tristram's imagined reader's question. (Tristram's mother asks if Walter Shandy has forgotten to wind up the clock and he replies, '*Good G——! . . . Did ever woman, since the creation of the world, interrupt a man with such a silly question?* Pray, what was your father saying?——Nothing' (Vol. 1, Ch. 1, p. 2/p. 5).) The primary function of this scene, however, is to suggest the comic frustrations in the Shandy marriage just as in a later scene Sterne uses a sexual reference in Uncle Toby's explanation for Mrs. Shandy's reluctance to be attended by the man-midwife as a springboard for characterization of both Uncle Toby, who doesn't 'know so much as the right end of a woman from the wrong', and Walter, who has a theory about this as about everything else (Vol. 2, Chs. 6 & 7, pp. 114–19/pp. 81–3).

In the next two volumes of *Tristram Shandy*, which appeared in January 1761, the influence of Rabelais and the comedy of reference is more strongly marked, in spite of Sterne's assertion after he had finished volume 3 that it contained 'more laughable humour,—with equal degree of Cervantik Satyr—if not more' than the first two volumes (*Letters*, pp. 120–21). Slawkenbergius's Tale and the extended equivocal passages about noses are comedy of reference, although in Rabelais the references are usually clear and direct, while in Sterne often much is left to the reader, as Sterne depends, ostensibly, 'upon the cleanliness of my reader's imaginations' (Vol. 3, Ch. 31, p. 258/p. 173). The incident with the hot chestnut which falls into 'the hiatus in Phutatorius's breeches' (Vol. 4, Ch. 27, p. 381/p. 257) is also Rabelaisian comedy, as is most of the Visitation Dinner. In characterizations of his book which recall Rabelais, Sterne says 'tis wrote . . . against the spleen', and it will promote true *Shandeism*, which 'opens the heart and lungs, . . . forces the blood and other vital fluids of the body to run freely thro' its channels, and makes the wheel of life run long and chearfully round' (Vol. 4, Ch. 22, p. 360/p. 239; Ch. 32, p. 401/p. 270). At the same time, the Cervantic gaps in communication between Walter and Toby continue, as do Walter's frustrations: 'not one single thing has gone right this day. . . . I would have sworn some retrograde planet was hanging over this unfortunate house of mine,' he says, 'and turning every individual thing in it out of its place' (Vol. 3, Ch. 23, p. 243/pp. 163–64). Finally, there is the Cervantic nimbleness of perspective:

> the circumstances with which every thing in this world is begirt, give every thing in this world its size and shape;—and by tightening it, or relaxing it, this way or that, make the thing to be, what it is—great—little—good—bad—indifferent or not indifferent, just as the case happens. (Vol. 3, Ch. 2, p. 187/ p. 126)

Toward the end of Volume 4 Sterne promises that in forthcoming instalments 'the amours of my uncle *Toby*, the events of which are of so singular a nature, and so Cervantick a cast', will bring him great credit as an author (Vol. 4, Ch. 32, p. 400/p. 269); and while he was writing Volumes 5 and 6, he wrote to a friend that he was so 'delighted with my uncle Toby's imaginary character, that I am become an enthusiast' (*Letters*, p. 143). In these two volumes there are still evident traces of Rabelais—in lists and catalogues, in a passage imitating the tuning of a fiddle (Vol. 5, Ch. 15), in the references to circumcision and the equivocal passages about whiskers, and in the various asterisks, only one group of which can be filled in with reasonable certainty.[14] But Sterne concentrates on the Cervantic comedy of character, the comedy of cross-purposes, as he rounds out the picture of the Shandy household. 'Though in one sense, our family was certainly a simple machine, as it consisted of a few wheels', he says,

> yet there was thus much to be said for it, that these wheels were set in motion by so many different springs, and acted one upon

the other from such a variety of strange principles and impulses,
—that though it was a simple machine, it had all the honour and
advantages of a complex one,—and a number of as odd
movements within it, as ever were beheld in the inside of a *Dutch*
silk-mill. (Vol. 5, Ch. 6, p. 427/p. 287)

This description precedes the passages telling how the news of
Bobby's death was received, with each person reacting not
even according to an obsession, but according to what was
'swimming uppermost in his own Brain'.[15] Likewise, the
discussion of Walter Shandy's Tristrapaedia, while it contains
Rabelaisian elements, is used mainly to give us a further
picture of Walter and his theories. A comparison with Slawkenbergius's tale, which is interrupted at length only once by a
return to the dramatic scene in which it is read, will illustrate
the difference: Slawkenbergius exists largely for its own
Rabelaisian sake, while the discussions of the Tristrapaedia
allow Sterne further to develop the interplay of character. The
description of Walter Shandy's bed of justice is a similar case.
The references to the context of sexual intercourse in the
words 'conceive', 'very short', 'pressing the point home to her',
are merely part of a dramatic scene which gives further
characterization of the colourless Mrs. Shandy and the frustrated Walter, who later says of his wife: 'That she is not a
woman of science . . . is her misfortune . . . but she might ask
a question' (Vol. 6, Ch. 18, pp. 526–29/pp. 351–53; Ch. 39,
p. 569/p. 378).

Tristram describes the Shandy world in terms that might
well be suited to tragedy: 'What a jovial and a merry world
would this be . . . but for that inextricable labyrinth of debts,
cares, woes, want, grief, discontent, melancholy, large jointures,
impositions, and lies!' (Vol. 6, Ch. 14, p. 520/p. 348). Yet this
'inextricable labyrinth' is seen comically and its inhabitants
survive the grief and frustration through their stoicism or their
goodness of heart. In the next *Shandy* we will see Tristram
himself engulfed in the labyrinth but facing it with laughter
and good will.

Volumes 7 and 8, published after a three-year hiatus while
Sterne sought health in travels on the Continent, have some
new departures. Volume 7 is an account of Tristram/Sterne's
travels, jumping from his childhood to the present; while

Volume 8 carries forward Uncle Toby's amours. Some of the Rabelaisian elements remain—passages with lists or strings of words or phrases, a passage or two with the stars or asterisks that Sterne used so lavishly in Volumes 5 and 6, passages with taboo words or sexual references or innuendos.[16] And in one passage Tristram says that he has put on his fool's cap (Vol. 7, Ch. 26, p. 616/p. 410). But the Cervantic elements are stronger, as the focus shifts in Volume 7 to Tristram, who sallies forth in a flight from Death, and in Volume 8 to Uncle Toby, who sallies forth on a 'campaign' to 'attack' the Widow Wadman. Tristram the narrator replaces Walter as the proto-type of comic frustration; the 'vexations' of his travels include being wakened from a sound sleep every six miles to pay carriage fare and being charged for changing his mind about the route he would take, having his chaise 'all broke to pieces' (Vol. 7, Ch. 29, p. 622/p. 414), and finding the principal sights of Lyons closed to view or misrepresented. The adult Tristram thus becomes a character whose presence is felt more clearly in the novel, and his comic troubles replace those of Walter Shandy to a large extent. He feels frustrations both 'as an author and a man', for he is constantly running into difficulties in his writing, he is in debt with 'ten cart-loads' of his fifth and sixth volumes as yet unsold, he is tormented with a 'vile asthma' and a broken vessel in his lungs, and he often suffers the same pangs of unrequited love as the Widow Wadman (Vol. 8, Chs. 6, 11). Yet he remains cheerful and, as Sterne had said in the first instalment, he lives 'in a constant endeavour to fence against the infirmities of ill health, and other evils of life, by mirth' (Dedication to Vols. 1 and 2; p. [3]). Writing—his hobby-horse, 'the sporting little filly-folly which carries you out for the present hour'—enables him 'to canter it away from the cares and solicitudes of life' (Vol. 8, Ch. 31, p. 716/p. 471).

The last instalment of *Tristram Shandy*—Volume 9—was published in 1767. The focus returns to the Shandy family and Uncle Toby's amours are concluded. Rabelaisian humour persists in puns, stars, strings of words, another brief fragment from Slawkenbergius, and various sexual references. Walter suggests a justification for the sexual references, pointing out the irony that we honour and speak freely about the 'act of killing and destroying a man' in war, while things connected with creating a human being 'are so held as to be conveyed to a cleanly mind by no language, translation, or periphrasis whatever' (Vol. 9, Ch. 33, p. 806/p. 538). At the same time the Cervantic strain continues, and Sterne invokes the 'Gentle Spirit of sweetest humour, who erst didst sit upon the easy pen of my beloved CERVANTES', while expressing a willingness to forego 'all the wit that ever *Rabelais* scatter'd', in telling the pathetic story of the mad Maria (Vol. 9, Ch. 24, pp. 780–84/ pp. 521–23). As Sterne includes more of the sentimental elements which will be central to *A Sentimental Journey*, he finds them more in harmony with Cervantes than with Rabelais. The amours of Uncle Toby also have their sentimental moments, but their mainspring lies in the gaps in communication between the Widow Wadman and Toby caused by his modesty and inexperience with women and her concupiscence, finally leading to an abandonment of his 'campaign'; and then the book ends with the *double entendre* of the Rabelaisian story of 'A COCK and a BULL' (Vol. 9, Ch. 33, p. 809/p. 539).

Though the proportions of Rabelaisian and Cervantic influence vary in the different parts of *Tristram Shandy*, Sterne has tried to maintain a balance between the two kinds of humour, and he often fuses them, as in the scenes where sexual references occur simultaneously with strokes of characterization. This balance and this fusion can be achieved because of the central position assumed by Tristram, the narrator, and the way he perceives the world. To alter Sterne's words slightly, it is almost 'like writing *himself* and not the *book*'. He sees a world in which there is much to thwart us but also much to laugh at with Rabelaisian gusto. It is also a world in which even Solomon, 'like all mortal men' has his 'ruling passion' (*Letters*, p. 89). Frustration and gaps in communication are inevitable, but the gaps can be bridged and the frustration endured because, as Walter and Toby agree, 'the best friends in the world may differ sometimes' (Vol. 2, Ch. 17, p. 155/ p. 106). Even 'in a world beset on all sides with mysteries and riddles' (Vol. 9, Ch. 22, p. 776/p. 517), laughter can triumph.

Laurence Sterne: Riddles and Mysteries

NOTES

1. *Letters*, p. 411.
2. *London Magazine*, xxix (February 1760), 111.
3. Sterne was familiar with the translation of Rabelais by Sir Thomas Urquhart and Peter Motteux as edited and revised by John Ozell in 1737. This translation has been reprinted in Everyman's Library, 2 vols. (London: J. M. Dent, 1929; rept. 1980) and I shall henceforth cite this reprint in the text, though it does not contain Ozell's notes, which Sterne sometimes drew upon, and it modernizes the capitalization of the original translation. Peter Motteux also translated Cervantes's *Don Quixote* and Ozell edited and revised this translation in 1719. It has been reprinted by the Modern Library (New York: Random House, 1950) and I shall henceforth cite this reprint in the text. (The same translation is also available in a reprint by Airmont, New York, 1967, with different pagination.)
4. Lewis Perry Curtis, *The Politicks of Laurence Sterne* (London: Oxford University Press, 1929), pp. 66, 70.
5. 'Philanthropy recommended', *Sermon III*, Vol. I, p. 51.
6. Lansing Van der Heyden Hammond, *Laurence Sterne's Sermons of Mr. Yorick* (New Haven: Yale University Press, 1948), p. 63.
7. 'The Levite and his Concubine', *Sermon III*, Vol. III, p. 70.
8. 'The Prodigal Son', *Sermon V*, Vol. III, p. 144.
9. '*Fragment Inédit*' in Paul Stapfer, *Laurence Sterne* (Paris: Ernest Thorin, 1870), pp. XLVIII, [XXII], XVIII–XX.
10. Laurence Sterne, *A Political Romance* (facsimile of 1759 edition) (Menston, Yorkshire, England: Scolar Press, 1971), p. 45.
11. Melvyn New, 'Sterne's Rabelaisian Fragment: A Text from the Holograph Manuscript' *P.M.L.A.*, LXXXVII (1972), 1083–92.
12. Ibid., p. 1088.
13. Ibid., p. 1089.
14. Sterne, *TS*, Vol. 5, Ch. 17, p. 449/p. 301, where the missing words seem to be 'chamber pot' and 'piss out of the window'.
15. See note 10 above.
16. See, for example, the talk about '*an old hat cock'd—and a cock'd old hat*' (Vol. 8, Ch. 10, p. 668/p. 443), the ass/arse pun (Vol. 8, Chs. 31–2, pp. 715–17/pp. 605–14), the stories of the Abbess of Andoüillets (Vol. 7, Chs. 20–5, pp. 605–14/pp. 403–9) and Trim and the Beguine (Vol. 8, Chs. 20–2, pp. 696–704/pp. 459–64).

4

'This Fragment of Life': From Process to Mortality

by EDWARD A. BLOOM and LILLIAN D. BLOOM

Contradicting most assumptions of the life process, Tristram Shandy's existence is a miracle of 'transverse zig-zaggery'.[1] As fictionalized biography, it is a grab-bag of dislocations, digressions, accidents and interruptions. For this hero, the span between life and death evokes an illusion of time during which mortality is but a moment in a flux of happenings— remembered, untrustworthy, superficially absurd:

> Could a historiographer drive on his history, as a muleteer drives on his mule,—straight forward; . . . he might venture to foretell you to an hour when he should get to his journey's end;——but the thing is, morally speaking, impossible: For, if he is a man of the least spirit, he will have fifty deviations from a straight line to make with this or that party as he goes along, which he can no ways avoid. (Vol. 1, Ch. 13, p. 41/p. 32)

Although the individual may attempt to control his progress toward dissolution, he must recognize that in the final analysis he cannot contravene the workings of fate. Yet he need not be dismayed by temporal decay; there is too much to be savoured of life in the process of moments and events which—because it has neither beginning nor ending—is perpetually new. Misfortune, ill health, and the like, as Sterne observed in his dedication to Pitt, must be met with good nature. '. . . every time a man smiles,—but much more so, when he laughs, [he] adds something to this Fragment of Life.'

Tristram himself is imbued with this spirit—an ironic one of self-deprecation and self-understanding—that gives him the courage to meet daily experience, for all of his comic ineptitude, with a perception that is altogether beyond the tortuous sophistry of Walter Shandy or the palpitant innocence of my uncle Toby.[2] Walter grieves:

> *But alas! . . . My Tristram's misfortunes began nine months before ever he came into the world.*——My mother, who was sitting by, look'd up,—but she knew no more than her backside what my father meant,—but my uncle . . . understood him very well. (Vol. 1, Ch. 3, p. 4/p. 7)

When Walter talks about bad luck, he is impervious to real emotion or altruism. When Toby weeps over bad luck, he does so without perceptible thought. The brothers, in short, are bemused witnesses. But Tristram, even as victim, is eager to engage in each episode contributing to the countless fragments of his life. If existence is for him an uncertain passage from one threat to the next, he neither cowers nor retreats nor despairs. He confronts the vicissitudes of destiny and flawed health without resentment or neurosis.

Both Tristram and his creator have a way of shrugging off each setback as a temporary disability that will soon be ameliorated. Tristram admits:

> I have been the continual sport of what the world calls Fortune; and though I will not wrong her by saying, She has ever made me feel the weight of any great or signal evil;—yet with all the good temper in the world, I affirm it of her, That in every stage of my life, and at every turn and corner where she could get fairly at me, the ungracious Duchess has pelted me with a set of as pitiful misadventures and cross accidents as ever small HERO sustained. (Vol. 1, Ch. 5, pp. 8–9/p. 10)

While Sterne concentrates Tristram's calamities for comic effect, he also extracts broader implications, representing through them the fallacy of expecting a life without pain or obstacle.

We are all vulnerable, he would have agreed with Samuel Johnson, to the truth 'that the misery of man proceeds not from any single crush of overwhelming evil, but from small vexations continually repeated'.[3] It is to this wry awareness that Tristram returns repeatedly as the 'Sport of small accidents . . . which have so often presented themselves in the course of [my] life' (Vol. 3, Ch. 8, p. 196/p. 132). Thus also he renews the image of a tyrannically 'ungracious Duchess', but still without rancour or self-pity. Hers, after all, were 'small evils' fit for a 'small HERO'. Bravely holding his ground, he declares: '. . . surely if I have any cause to be angry with her, 'tis that she has not sent me any great [evils]—a score of good cursed, bouncing losses, would have been as good as a pension to me' (Vol. 7, Ch. 29, p. 624/p. 415). Denied even the singularity of any major catastrophe (as it might be viewed outside of his immediate circle of family and friends), he can proceed in his own maladroit way only to 'VEXATION upon VEXATION' (Vol. 7, Ch. 30, p. 625/p. 416). One of the beguiling traits of Tristram is the picaresque resilience that allows him to rebound from disaster even while airily mocking himself. Consummate clown, victim of parental eccentricity and misunderstanding, he carries his burdens with a cheerfulness made credible only by Sterne's artistry. Despite the bad omens of prenatal miscalculation, baptismal error, involuntary circumcision—among other 'small vexations'—Tristram remains unfailingly jaunty. No less a jester than Parson Yorick, he too exudes *gaité de coeur* and like him is of a 'mercurial and sublimated . . . composition' (Vol. 1, Ch. 11, p. 27/p. 22).

In order to emphasize the vagaries besetting his eccentrics, Sterne occasionally resorts to gambling metaphors: *dice, doublets, cast*.[4] Even more overtly, and in his most affective manner, he relies upon narrative situation and statement. Thus, that inveterate talker Walter is obsessed with the notion of capricious destiny, as when he attributes differences in human understanding to 'the lucky or unlucky organization of the body, in that part where the soul principally took up her residence' (Vol. 2, Ch. 19, p. 173/p. 117). And, although sorely tried by a naïvely obtrusive Toby, Walter nevertheless goes on to warn his brother about 'the accidents which unavoidably way-lay [children]' in their procreation and in errant processes of experience. An impressed uncle Toby whistles *Lillabullero* without knowing that the whimsical, prescient fates have been promoting his own 'good' fortune. Unaccountably benign, '(and with more courtesy than they usually do things of this kind)', they had 'established . . . a chain of causes and effects' that was to make connection with the Widow Wadman inescapable (Vol. 8, Ch. 14, p. 673/p. 445). Meanwhile, Trim for his part was convinced that his own rather less disabling wound was a gift of the gods who in this way reserved him to serve Toby and to be cared for by him, an act of benevolent freakishness that deeply moved the two old soldiers. Every occurrence, they mutually infer, is 'a matter of contingency, which might happen, or not, just as chance' decrees (Vol. 8, Ch. 19, p. 693/p. 457).

Sometimes in this Shandean universe man is represented as duped by a temporal whimsy that can be crueller and no more comprehensible than that which is supernally imposed. Through the persona of Yorick, notably, the reader enters a generally hidden state in which laughter veils the pain of injustice and intolerance. An idealized worldling, Parson Yorick could 'meditate as delightfully *de vanitate mundi et fugâ saeculi*, as with the advantage of a death's head before him' (Vol. 1, Ch. 10, p. 20/p. 18). A good man who loved a joke, even at his own expense, he was still a butt of malice and ridicule, subject to

> a fatality [that] attends the actions of some men: Order them as they will, they pass thro' a certain medium, which so twists and refracts them from their true directions——that, with all the titles to praise which a rectitude of heart can give, the doers of them are nevertheless forced to live and die without it. (Vol. 1, Ch. 10, p. 24/p. 20)

Such was the destiny of Yorick, whose pathetic death comes after a long and valiant struggle to withstand the maulings of his enemies. As described by Eugenius, he was finally overpowered not only by numbers but by the harsh ungenerosity of repeated attack. Thus, 'he threw down the sword; and though he kept up his spirits in appearance to the last,—he died nevertheless, as was generally thought, quite broken hearted' (Vol. 1, Ch. 12, p. 33/p. 26). Deliberate finite malice, ironically, may be more damaging to the human spirit than seemingly cosmic, if random, afflictions. Betrayal of brotherhood, to apply Sterne's humane credo, is less bearable than are the scattered blows of the rude, indiscriminate duchess. Whatever the base, however—temporal or teleological—Sterne consistently relates mortal being to a struggle for accommodation. In an unknowable scheme pervaded by the accidental and unpredictable and trivial, the fulfilment of aspiration is at least a stumbling possibility.

Significantly, Tristram the fallible observer and feckless *schlemiel* refuses to speculate on causes that are entirely beyond human ken. As a manipulated character he chooses, rather, 'to point out to the curious, different tracts of investigation, to come at the first springs of the events I tell . . . with the officious humility of a heart devoted to the assistance merely of the inquisitive' (Vol. 1, Ch. 21, p. 74/p. 54). Here, despite a pretence of naïve inadequacy, he is made to understate, slyly goading us into perceptions that lurk beneath the shrewdly deployed 'tracts of investigation'. More the omniscient storyteller than his protesting narrator lets on, Sterne uses him to enforce narrative and thematic strategy. Whether providing a Shandean genealogy or reporting the tragedies of Bobby and Le Fever, Sterne urges us to respond as if witnessing familiar experiences. Along the way he discloses a gallery of originals who, despite the distortions of caricature, are seldom without human dimension. Sterne's creative vision is deceptively antic, for it is always regulated by reason and attuned—however opaquely—to social reality.

That reality, it should be noted, was as much in the domain of Sterne the clergyman as of Sterne the novelist, an obvious assumption for anyone who has sampled the *Sermons*. The theological discourses are often concerned with the same questions about mortal indeterminacy as frame *Tristram Shandy*. *Sermon V*, for instance, is a plea for charity that the preacher hopes will be a bulwark against 'the great instability of temporal affairs, and constant fluctuations of everything in this world'. More pointedly, *Sermon X* muses on 'Troubles of Life' with the rhetorical question: 'Do not ten thousand accidents break off the slender thread of human life, long before it can be drawn out' to its full threescore and ten? 'The hopeful youth in the very pride and beauty of his life is cut off; some cruel distemper or unthought-of accident lays him prostrate upon the earth, to pursue Job's comparison [14:2 ff.], like a blooming flower smit and shrivelled up with a malignant blast.' Again invoking Job [2:10], in *Sermon XV* Sterne warns rigorously against the dangers of complacency in a life that is 'fickle and capricious'. But he also reminds his auditors that they should confront these hazards with Christian fortitude, since they stem from 'wise reasons' known only to God.[5]

The *Sermons* are of course formal pronouncements addressed to specific occasions. The sombreness of tone, appropriate enough for a church service, contrasts with the bantering good nature of the fiction. Yet there is no denying the thematic parallel which informs the words uttered from the pulpit and inscribed in the novel. And sometimes, as when Sterne in *Sermon VIII* draws the text of 'Time and Chance' from Ecclesiastes 9:11, the lines between sermon and novel begin to converge even more closely.

> When a man casts a look upon this melancholy description of the world, and sees, contrary to all his guesses and expectations, what different fates attend the lives of men, . . . he is apt to conclude with a sigh upon it,——in the words,——though not in the sense of the wise man,——That time and chance happeneth to them all——That time and chance,——apt seasons and fit conjectures have the greatest sway, in the turns and disposals of men's fortunes. And that, as these lucky hits (as they are called) happen to be for, or against a man,—they either open the way to his advancement against all obstacles,— or block it up against all helps and attempts.[6]

Sonorous sentiments these are, as suitable for Parson Yorick or, for that matter, Corporal Trim, as for the Reverend Mr. Sterne. Linked with the characteristic phrases and appositions, they recall the self-conscious gestures and hesitations of the fiction; they exploit biblical apothegm in a reasoned context which confirms man's uneasy relationship to destiny.

In a narrative setting where nothing can be depended upon but accident, Sterne deliberately creates an impression that violates many cherished assumptions of order, ratiocination and social intercourse. Opposed to them, and congruous with the theory of fortuity that shapes his reaction to reality, he weaves a complex network of digression, involution and interruption. Thus he subverts the security that most of us seek in conventional patterns of conduct and thought. The

truth of actuality, as he would have it, is summed up in Parson
Yorick's candid admission: 'I am governed by circumstances—
I cannot govern them.' Just moments before, he had conceded:
'I think there is a fatality [in my restless searchings]—I
seldom go to the place I set out for' (*SJ*, p. 208). His actions,
like those of all Shandeans, seem spontaneous, undirected. But
dexterously the author orchestrates events to epitomize the
principle of the helter-skelter expressed by Yorick. Contrarily,
'To prescribe system to Sterne', one early admirer had
mistakenly conjectured, 'really seemed to us like teaching a
humming-bird to fly according to mathematics.' Surely we no
longer need apologize for his 'delightful wildness' or share
Samuel Richardson's hostile correlative, a fear of 'being
poisoned with disgustful nonsense'.[7] The disarray that often
perplexes Sterne's readers is, paradoxically, arranged so for
artistic and thematic effect.

Within the planned maze of mischance and crossed purposes, there exists a potential bond of kinship. Or to change
the image, as in an intricate dance, various characters are
brought into conjunction, although without patent methodized
cause. Consistently inconsistent in their comings and goings,
they are allowed at unexpected junctures to disappear from
sight only to re-emerge dozens or hundreds of pages later as
though never absent. Strangers as familiar as old friends
validate Yorick's 'conviction of consanguinity . . . Tut! said I,
are we not all relations?' (*SJ*, p. 191). These are circumstantial
associations, hoped for perhaps but no more anticipated than
any random encounter, and durable or not—as chance orders.
Yorick perceives of himself:

> 'Tis going . . . like the Knight of the Woeful Countenance, in
> Quest of melancholy adventures—but I know not how it is, but
> I am never so perfectly conscious of the existence of a soul
> within me, as when I am entangled in them. (*SJ*, p. 270)

Intuitive if not easily articulated, brotherhood is the constant
that should matter in an otherwise disjunctive condition. The
dilemma for most of Sterne's folk, however, is that only rarely
can they transcend themselves. Locked into their egos, they
barely make connections with the exterior world, dealing only
with isolated particulars.

What are we to expect other than discontinuity and incoherence when basic conversation between two speakers as often as not deteriorates into a succession of *non-sequiturs?* The frequency of dissociative situations is Sterne's comic caution to be wary of assurances about causal logic. Paradoxically no doubt, but also metaphorically, his fiction reveals few bridges between primary cause and temporal effect, between the spoken word and the irrelevant response. Sterne points to evident causes 'of obscurity and confusion, in the mind of man': these are chiefly physiological, that is, 'Dull organs . . . slight and transient impressions made by objects . . . a memory like unto a sieve' (Vol. 2, Ch. 2, p. 99/p. 70). But he virtually dismisses the sensory and mnemonic as genuinely efficient causes of confusion and incompatibility, implying that they are trivial by comparison with the unreliability of language.

Herein is a *leitmotiv* of his fiction. Fluctuating haphazardly, Sterne's people seldom achieve fixed relationships.

> ——How, in the name of wonder! could your uncle *Toby*, who, it seems, was a military man, and whom you have represented as no fool,—be at the same time such a confused, pudding-headed, muddle-headed fellow . . . What [the origin is], I have hinted above, and a fertile source of obscurity it is,—and ever will be,—and that is the unsteady uses of words which have perplexed the clearest and most exalted under-standings. (Vol. 2, Ch. 2, pp. 97–100/pp. 69–71)

Afflicted by a kind of verbal paralysis—or at best of syntactic illogicality—the characters define the duration and space in which they coexist. Only vaguely cohesive, they constitute degrees and forms of singularity that distance them from custom and enclose them in their own odd mould. Yet even within this enclosure, they are further isolated, separated one from the other by barriers of language. Unable to communicate any measurable part of their inner selves, always guarding essential traits, moved every which way by chance, they remain forever dissociated.[8]

Although Walter misreads a book on parturition, he is able to reach the apt conclusion, 'that so many of our best heads are no better than a puzzled skein of silk,—all perplexity,—all confusion within-side' (Vol. 2, Ch. 19, p. 177). Then, to compound an error which has led to this tangential awareness, Tristram as narrator is reproached by the author for having named the wrong book (Vol. 2, Ch. 19, p. 176n/p. 119n).[9] Built into the episode is an anticipation of that most disastrous of all namings, the accidental shift from Trismegistus to Tristram, thanks to an uncomprehending Susannah (Vol. 4, Ch. 14, pp. 343–44/pp. 229–30). My uncle Toby's verbal resources become equally involuted when he attempts to explain the military subtleties affecting the siege of Namur, where he received the famous wound. Inevitably the complex 'clarification' slips so far out of his grasp that he 'did oft times puzzle his visiters; and sometimes himself too . . . 'twas a difficult thing, do what he could, to keep the discourse free from obscurity' (Vol. 2, Ch. 1, p. 94/p. 67). Progressively frustrated by the breakdown of language, Toby withdraws to the privacy of obsessive memories. These are to become a comfortable sanctuary—the essence of his hobby-horse—but only when he is able to order and re-live his military experiences with the aid of symbolic, albeit arbitrary, configurations of a map.[10] Only the faithful Corporal Trim, who has witnessed those events, can find an entrance into Toby's barricaded, reconstructed past. And even this mutuality evolves from involuntary empathy rather than conscious understanding, from a profound desire to serve (thereby subordinating the self) rather than to share.

Nowhere does Sterne exemplify more graphically than in the news of Bobby's death the spiritual as well as verbal distance between individuals. So absorbed is Walter in estimating the expenses of his son's travels, that he is totally bewildered by the greater actuality:

> ——he's gone! said my uncle *Toby*.—Where—Who? cried my father.—My nephew, said my uncle *Toby*.——What—without leave—without money——without governor? cried my father in amazement. No:—he is dead, my dear brother, quoth my uncle *Toby*.—Without being ill? cried my father again. . . .
> (Vol. 5, Ch. 2, p. 417/p. 281)

Encased in his egocentric shell, Walter cannot respond emotively—or, indeed, relevantly—to an event of such mortal and parental significance. The abrupt termination of a young life, the break in family continuity, these pale by comparison with the opportunity for an unconnected harangue on death and eternity. In Walter's insulated mind, death is an acceptable abstraction, an occasion for quasi-philosophic rhetoric divorced from the specific instance of loss ('he had absolutely forgot my brother *Bobby*') (Vol. 5, Ch. 3, p. 425/p. 286). As another example of obtuse egoism, Susannah reacts to the same event in an altogether different way. Initially she leaps to a mildly prurient association between Bobby's death and her mistress's green satin nightgown, evoking Tristram's interpolation, 'Well might *Locke* write a chapter upon the imperfections of words' (Vol. 5, Ch. 7, p. 429/p. 288).[11] Then there is Trim, already a proven orator, who rises to the solemnity engendered by the sad news with an affecting though generalized discourse on human frailty. Unable to depend on reverential words alone, he abets them with the symbolic gesture of the dropped hat. It fell 'as if a heavy lump of clay had been kneaded into the crown of it.——Nothing could have expressed the sentiment of mortality, of which it was the type and forerunner, like it . . .' (Vol. 5, Ch. 7, p. 432/ p. 290).[12]

The Shandean concept of being shuttles intricately between poles of opposition and reconciliation, of disparateness and fusion, of cosmic schemes that have been termed 'open' and 'closed'. The last is subject to some regulatory force that preordains all events. The other, an 'open' scheme, is a wanton one in which everything is accidental, inadvertent.[13] Contrarieties that seemingly defy all rational principles, and ever-present imbalances of magnitude and diminution, these allow us along with Tristram to account only for fragmented effects. But somewhere within the labyrinthine puzzle is a primary cause responsible for invisible strands of harmonious confusion.[14] Subscribing to the Coleridgean thesis of finite triviality juxtaposed to infinite consequence, McKillop concludes that the Shandaic

> universe is pictured as a great multiple system, in which sense and spirit, macrocosm and microcosm, are linked by analogies and correspondences, and also as a great dynamic system to be

studied in terms of cause and effect. Causality lends itself to the
same kind of play with great and small, the great cause and the
trivial effect, the minute cause and the great effect.[15]

As the mirror of Sterne's skewed way of looking at the
phenomenal and beyond, the narrative may be disquieting if
we reject the possibility of an implicit order underlying and
thus contiguous with the surface meanderings. Many of his
readers have balked at the dizzying turns, bends, and
inversions, at his refusal to be conventional and follow a direct
line of time and event. And yet, throughout the erratic
movements of the 'plot', he has marshalled all of the ingredients
essential to causal connections.

Enclosed or open, the eccentric space invented by this
mosaicist asserts its basic substance, to confirm that 'the world
was *there*, with some solidity'.[16] Because everyone must pass
through it between birth and death, Sterne re-creates dominant
impressions as though from the conveniently familiar perspectives of travellers. It is by no means a morbid journey during
which the principal wanderers, Tristram and Yorick, live
fully, that is to say, with maximum sensuous dedication to an
élan vital. Yorick has no doubt that only luck will determine
whether anything useful can be acquired from an organized
programme of travel (*SJ*, p. 84). But he is equally convinced
that, however randomly, extraordinary riches await anyone
who will take the trouble to reach out for them as they happen
to come this way. He pities 'the man who can travel from *Dan*
to *Beersheba*, and cry, 'Tis all barren—and so it is; and so is all
the world to him who will not cultivate the fruits it offers' (*SJ*,
p. 115). Sterne pleaded in his own voice,

> we may surely be allowed to amuse ourselves with the natural
> or artificial beauties of the country we are passing through,
> without reproach of forgetting the main errand we are sent
> upon.[17]

Despite outward signs of epicurean indulgence, Sterne was
a good Christian and a clergyman for whom the life of realized
action was infinitely preferable to one of self-satisfying lamen-
tation such as Walter's (ironically sounded by the narrator):
'What is the life of man! Is it not to shift from side to side?—
from sorrow to sorrow?——to button up one cause of

vexation!—and unbutton another!' (Vol. 4, Ch. 31, p. 399/
p. 268).[18] In allegory or fact, Sterne would have contended,
once the joy of the mortal journey has dissipated, then life itself
dissolves into meaninglessness. Vigorously he declared himself
against the abjuration of Ecclesiastes 7:2,3—'It is better to go
to the house of mourning than to the house of feasting.' Not so
in Sterne's philosophy, except perhaps 'for a crack-brain'd
order of Carthusian monks'.[19] Laughter, he urged, is always
better than the stupefying emotion of grief. Sorrow arrests the
mind and feelings, whereas laughter is regenerative, inducing
a constructive outlook on events and people. As a related
source of animation, the creative imagination repudiates self-
pity and the banality of idle phrases. Thus we see how Parson
Yorick, through the vicarious agency of literature, renews and
rediscovers himself.

> When my way is too rough for my feet, or too steep for my
> strength, I get off it, to some smooth velvet path which fancy
> has scattered over with rose-buds of delights; and having taken
> a few turns in it, come back strengthen'd and refresh'd—When
> evils press sore upon me, and there is no retreat from them in
> this world, then I take a new course—I leave it—and as I have
> a clearer idea of the Elysian fields than I have of heaven, I force
> myself, like Eneas, into them—I see him meet the pensive
> shade of his forsaken Dido . . . I lose the feelings for myself in
> hers. . . .
> I can safely say for myself, I was never able to conquer any
> one single bad sensation in my heart so decisively, as by beating
> up as fast as I could for some kindly and gentle sensation, to
> fight it upon its own ground. (*SJ*, pp. 225–26)

Parson Yorick yearns to be convinced that the flux and
dissociation of mortal affairs may in fact be illusory. His lyrical
musings, surely, are conditional upon the hope of a cohesive,
finer certainty—in his case, the solace of creative beauty
invested with a sub-sensuous link to all of mankind, past,
present, and future. There is a correspondence here with
Sterne's celebrated theory of digression, which the narrator
treats not as a rambling shift in storytelling direction but,
rather, as a vital pause during which the overt business of the
fiction is suspended, if only to be filled with other, obliquely
related matter. These intervals of arrested central action play

upon the senses somewhat like the rests of a musical passage, each designed to generate a special kind of tension. The rhythmic silence is a momentary break in time to intensify emotions. Sterne's digressions likewise interrupt the flow of time in part to mock unquestioning trust in causal inevitability. But experience tells us also that in due course the unheard music and the restrained action will be reactivated, set in place once again where they belong in the conscious scheme of time and space.

> For, if [the author] begins a digression,—from that moment, I observe, his whole work stands stock-still;—and if he goes on with his main work,——then there is an end of his digression.

The concept is paradoxical, but only if we insist upon digression as a competing or diversionary movement—literally, that is, a turning aside, a detour from the primary road. Despite Sterne's intimation of stasis, he means us to know that calendar time is irrelevant only for the digressive occasion, but that it continues its inevitable advance free of empiric considerations at a sub-narrative level. For structural convenience he causes the interpolated event or opinion to supersede present time somewhat as memory recalls associations that then impinge upon conscious perception. 'Digressions', he proclaims, 'incontestably, are the sun-shine . . . the life, the soul of reading.' As such, they are symptomatic of the way in which he interprets experience. Although the tempo of existence is constantly deregulated because of the distractions which impede prospects for a smooth journey, life does go forward, and inexorably. Creatively, 'two contrary motions are introduced into [the fiction], and reconciled, which were thought to be at variance with each other. In a word, my work is digressive, and it is progressive too,—and at the same time.' The paradox of 'progressive digression' is a Shandean imperative, an elastic resolution of puzzling disparities whereby phenomenal oppositions of time and place become comprehensible. Ultimately at issue are unification of history and the moment, absorption of varied experiences into a single one of common value and meaning.

> ——This is vile work.—For which reason, from the beginning of this, you see, I have constructed the main work and the

adventitious parts of it with such intersections, and have so complicated and involved the digressive and progressive movements, one wheel within another, that the whole machine, in general, has been kept a-going;—and, what's more, it shall be kept a-going these forty years, if it pleases the fountain of health to bless me so long with life and good spirits. (Vol. 1, Ch. 22, pp. 81–2/pp. 58–9)

The 'machine', as Tristram calls it, connotes among other things his ridicule of life's tenuity.[20] By comparison with myriad manifestations of durability, the body is a reminder of its own impermanence. Arguably, death is the final reality; for although it is the end of one journey, even that finality is inconclusive. Existence without hope of futurity, Sterne the parson intimates, in *Sermon XII*, Vol. 6, 'Eternal Advantages of Religion', is a void. Death cannot be comprehended through rational, transcendent, or arbitrary terms of dispute. The logician in 'Slawkenbergius's Tale', for instance, defines it as 'being nothing but the stagnation of the blood'. His antagonist, however, takes the metaphysical tack that 'Death is the separation of the soul from the body' (Vol. 4, p. 309/p. 207). They agree only that they cannot agree and therefore cannot go on with the exchange. And that is the point about death, as precisely as Sterne can bring himself to enunciate it: however hard one tries, there is no way to account for it. One may submit, as Trim does with conventional eloquence inspired by the metaphor of flesh returned to earth. But almost instantly his audience are distracted by 'the scullion [who] had just been scouring a fish-kettle.—It was not fair.——' (Vol. 5, Ch. 9, p. 435/p. 292). The unexpectedness and democracy of death are brought home forcefully by the abrupt authorial lament for the corporal—'Tread lightly on his ashes, ye men of genius,——for he was your kinsman' (Vol. 6, Ch. 25, p. 544/p. 362). In both comic and sentimental fact, Sterne plays havoc with time, anticipating the distant funereal event in a present context. And soon thereafter, as a further conflation of death and life, he prepares us in earnest for the courtship of my uncle Toby and the Widow Wadman (Vol. 6, Chs. 35–7).

The dominant pattern of the fiction, then, may be visualized as a crosshatch of movements in which death, an ultimately prevailing entity, intersects life. The 'small HERO', however,

refuses to capitulate. When ill health increasingly underscores
the hopelessness of his mortal state, he asserts defiance in a
spirit reminiscent of Donne's challenge to death, 'be not proud
. . . nor yet canst thou kill me'. Sterne's narrator is simultaneously impudent and gallant:

> . . . when DEATH himself knocked at my door—ye bad him
> come again; and in so gay a tone of careless indifference, did ye
> do it, that he doubted of his commission——.(Vol. 7, Ch. 1,
> p. 576/p. 385)

> . . . I had left Death, the lord knows——and He only—how far
> behind me——'I have followed many a man thro' France,
> quoth he—but never at this mettlesome rate'——Still he
> followed,——and still I fled him——but I fled him chear-
> fully——still he pursued—but like one who pursued his prey
> without hope——as he lag'd, every step he lost, softened his
> looks——why should I fly him at this rate? (Vol. 7, Ch. 42,
> p. 645/p. 428)

Tristram Shandy at this point could well have said in the
words of his mortally ill creator, 'I feel the principle of life
strong within me.'[21]

NOTES

1. *TS*, Vol. 3, Ch. 3, p. 189/p. 127.
2. See John M. Stedmond, 'Tristram as Clown', *The Comic Art of Laurence Sterne: Convention and Innovation in 'Tristram Shandy' and 'A Sentimental Journey'* (Toronto: University of Toronto Press, 1967), pp. 66–131; Wayne C. Booth, *The Rhetoric of Fiction* (Chicago: University of Chicago Press, 1961), pp. 230–33.
3. 'Pope', *Lives of the English Poets*, ed. George Birkbeck Hill (Oxford: Oxford University Press, 1905), Vol. 3, p. 234.
4. Cf. *TS*, Vol. 2, Ch. 5, p. 108/p. 76; *SJ* pp. 136–37.
5. 'Elijah and the Widow', *Sermon V*, Vol. 1, p. 130; 'Job's Account of the Shortness and troubles of life, considered', *Sermon X*, Vol. 2, p. 94; 'Job's expostulation with his wife', *Sermon XV*, Vol. 2, p. 237.
6. 'Time and Chance', *Sermon VIII*, Vol. 2, p. 27. Cf. 'Eternal Advantages of Religion', *Sermon XII*, Vol. 6. For Sterne's obligations to John Tillotson, Samuel Clarke, and other English divines, see Lansing Van der Heyden Hammond, *Laurence Sterne's Sermons of Mr. Yorick* (New Haven: Yale University Press, 1948), pp. 74–89.

7. Extracts from the American periodical *Port Folio* (1811) and a letter of Richardson to Bishop Mark Hildesley (1761), in *Sterne: The Critical Heritage*, ed. Alan B. Howes (London: Routledge and Kegan Paul, 1974), pp. 340 and 129.
8. Among those who have written on Sterne's concern with language, see: John Traugott, *Tristram Shandy's World: Sterne's Philosophical Rhetoric* (Berkeley and Los Angeles: University of California Press, 1954); Stedmond, pp. 30–47; Henri Fluchère, *Laurence Sterne: From Tristram to Yorick*, trans. and abr. by Barbara Bray (Oxford: Oxford University Press, 1965), pp. 58–64, *et passim*; William V. Holtz, *Image and Immortality: A Study of Tristram Shandy* (Providence: Brown University Press, 1970), pp. 65–89.
9. See editor's comment (p. 556), World's Classics edition, on the satiric intention of the rebuke.
10. 'The hobby-horse', according to Fluchère (p. 140), 'is a certain refuge against the caprices of the outside world.'
11. John Locke, *E.C.H.U.*, Bk. 3, Ch. 9.
12. See *Coleridge's Miscellaneous Criticism*, ed. Thomas Middleton Raysor (Cambridge: Harvard University Press, 1936), p. 444; extracts in *The Critical Heritage*, pp. 353–58; and Dorothy Van Ghent, *The English Novel: Form and Function* (New York: Rinehart & Co., 1953), pp. 94–5.
13. A. A. Mendilow argues for the 'open-closed' juxtaposition, in Arthur H. Cash and John M. Stedmond (eds.), *The Winged Skull: Papers from the Laurence Sterne Bicentenary Conference* (Kent, Ohio: Kent State University Press, 1971), pp. 83–4.
14.   Not Chaos-like together crush'd and bruis'd,
            But, as the world, harmoniously confus'd:
                    —Alexander Pope, *Windsor-Forest*, ll. 13–14.
15. Alan Dugald McKillop, *The Early Masters of English Fiction* (Lawrence: University of Kansas Press, 1956), p. 198.
16. Jean-Jacques Mayoux, in *The Winged Skull*, p. 78.
17. 'The House of Feasting and the House of Mourning described', *Sermon II*, Vol. 1, p. 27.
18. Cf. 'Eternal Advantages of Religion': 'take notice of the several accidents of life', *Sermon XII*, Vol. 6, p. 157 *et passim*.
19. *Sermon II*, Vol. I, p. 24.
20. For an interesting interpretation of the 'machine', see McKillop, pp. 201–3.
21. Sterne writing to Elizabeth Draper, March 1767. *Letters*, p. 320.

Part Two:

THE INTELLECTUAL
BACKGROUND

5

Tristram Shandy: Locke May Not Be the Key

by W. G. DAY

The annotations to *Tristram Shandy* in the Florida edition of Sterne's works list well over two hundred occasions when Sterne is indebted to an identifiable source for his choice of words.[1] Many of these instances are covert, there being no indication of Sterne's immediate source; some are quite open: to the second edition of Volume 1 for example he added the footnote providing details of the 'Mémoire' of the Doctors of the Sorbonne (p. 67/p. 49). Of these open borrowings many are quite unobjectionable; the original words are used with only such changes as were necessary to incorporate them into the context, and there are often references to author or a well known character from the source book, and occasionally typographical indicators, italics or inverted commas. Such is Sterne's technique with, for example, Rabelais and Cervantes.

With Locke it is different. A good deal has been written about Sterne's indebtedness to Locke in such areas as his time scheme and the progression of the narrative;[2] not a great deal of attention has been paid to Sterne's verbal rather than conceptual borrowings from Locke in *Tristram Shandy*. In *Laurence Sterne's Sermons of Mr. Yorick* Hammond identified passages where Sterne was verbally indebted to Locke's *Essay Concerning Human Understanding*, *Some Thoughts Concerning Education*, and *The Reasonableness of Christianity*.[3] The two latter do not seem to have contributed to *Tristram Shandy*, where there have so far been identified eight passages from *E.C.H.U.* and two from *Two Treatises of Government.*

One may assume that the intelligent contemporary reader of *Tristram Shandy* had read *E.C.H.U.* and was reasonably conversant with its argument. In Waterland's *Advice to a Young Student*, which was circulating in Cambridge when Sterne was up, a note to the scheme of reading for the second year said quite bluntly, 'Locke's Human Understanding must be read',[4] and Kenneth MacLean's *John Locke and English Literature of the Eighteenth Century* (New Haven: Yale University Press, 1936) demonstrates how all-pervasive Locke's ideas, and words, were. It is this assumption, of the reader's detailed knowledge of Locke, which is vital to any discussion of Sterne's use of his works.

With few exceptions, when borrowings are made from Locke there is an effective alteration or addition to the original wording. The effect is not a constant one; Sterne's attitude to Locke's writing appears to have been equivocal. The first reference to Locke comes in Volume I, Chapter 4. Basing his ideas upon Locke's,

> This wrong Connexion in our Minds of *Ideas* in themselves, loose and independent one of another, has such an influence, and is of so great force to set us awry in our Actions, as well Moral as Natural, Passions, Reasonings, and Notions themselves, that, perhaps, there is not any one thing that deserves more to be looked after,[5]

Sterne wrote,

> . . . from an unhappy association of ideas which have no connection in nature, it so fell out at length, that my poor mother could never hear the said clock wound up,—but the thoughts of some other things unavoidably popp'd into her head,—& *vice versâ*:—which strange combination of ideas, the sagacious *Locke*, who certainly understood the nature of these things better than most men, affirms to have produced more wry actions than all other sources of prejudice whatsoever. (p. 7/p. 9)

At first reading this seems complimentary: Locke is a 'sagacious' man 'who certainly understood the nature of these things better than most men'. But what are 'these things'? Is the reference to 'ideas', or is it to Mrs. Shandy's 'other things'? Equivocation is established from the outset. The reader who may have had some doubt about Sterne's position *vis-à-vis* Locke raised at this point will find these doubts hardened when, in the second chapter of Volume 2, he comes across a bravura performance based very closely upon *E.C.H.U.* Locke made his point quite clearly:

> The *cause of Obscurity* in simple *Ideas*, seems to be either dull Organs; or very slight and transient Impressions made by the Objects; or else a weakness in the Memory, not able to retain them as received. For to return again to visible Objects, to help us apprehend this matter. If the Organs, or Faculties of Perception, like Wax overhardned with Cold, will not receive the Impression of the Seal, from the usual impulse wont to imprint it; or, like Wax of a temper too soft, will not hold it well, when well imprinted; or else supposing the Wax of a temper fit, but the Seal not applied with a sufficient force, to make a clear Impression: In any of these cases, the print left by the Seal, will be *obscure*. This, I suppose, needs no application to make it plainer. (II, xxix, §3, 363–64)

Sterne is so extravagant in his variations on this passage that even the 'unlearned reader' might have cause to suspect his intentions. Sterne opens the sequence in a way which suggests he is about to praise Locke very much in the way he praises Hogarth several pages later:

> Pray, Sir, in all the reading which you have ever read, did you ever read such a book as *Locke*'s Essay upon the Human Understanding?—Don't answer me rashly,—because many, I know, quote the book, who have not read it,—and many have read it who understand it not . . . it will be found that the cause of obscurity and confusion, in the mind of man, is threefold.
> Dull organs, dear Sir, in the first place. Secondly, slight and transient impressions made by objects when the said organs are not dull. And, thirdly, a memory like unto a sieve, not able to retain what it has received—Call down *Dolly* your chambermaid, and I will give you my cap and bell along with it, if I make not this matter so plain that *Dolly* herself shall understand it as well as *Malbranch*.—When *Dolly* has indited her epistle to *Robin*, and has thrust her arm into the bottom of her pocket hanging by her right side;—take that opportunity to recollect that the organs and faculties of perception, can, by nothing in

this world, be so aptly typified and explained as by that one thing which *Dolly*'s hand is in search of.—Your organs are not so dull that I should inform you—'tis an inch, Sir, of red seal-wax.

When this is melted and dropp'd upon the letter, if *Dolly* fumbles too long for her thimble, till the wax is over-harden'd, it will not receive the mark of her thimble from the usual impulse which was wont to imprint it. Very well: If *Dolly*'s wax, for want of better, is bees-wax, or of a temper too soft,—tho' it may receive,—it will not hold the impression, how hard soever *Dolly* thrusts against it; and last of all, supposing the wax good, and eke the thimble, but applied thereto in careless haste, as her Mistress rings the bell;—in any one of these three cases, the print, left by the thimble, will be as unlike the prototype as a brass-jack. (pp. 98–9/pp. 70–1)

Sterne ridicules Locke by the comic translation of his illustration from the general to the specific. Locke's simile is quite acceptable in its context, but by passing slighting comment upon the lightness of the image in relation to the text ('. . . the organs and faculties of perception, can, by nothing in this world, be so aptly typified and explained as by . . . an inch, Sir, of red seal-wax'), by identifying Locke's wax as Dolly's wax, and by introducing the element of innuendo in the description of Dolly's searching fingers, the original is transformed. And the transformation is made more ludicrous for the knowledgeable reader, in the circumstances, by Locke's almost pathetic conclusion, 'This, I suppose, needs no application to make it plainer.' There are at least two levels of humorous reaction. The one is to the unnecessary length and complexity of the image Sterne creates, even to the introduction of Dolly's mistress ringing the bell. This reaction is enhanced by the further comment, 'Now you must understand that not one of these was the true cause of the confusion . . .' (p. 100/p. 71). The other is to the extent and nature of Sterne's perversion of his original.

After this performance Sterne's next borrowing from *E.C.H.U.* is very muted: a brief and quite acceptable resumé of Locke's 'Of duration and its simple modes', which is followed by Walter Shandy's lengthy explanation to his brother of the concepts of time, duration and the association of ideas. That this is a specific verbal borrowing is made absolutely clear. Much of Walter's opening peroration is italicized, a device used elsewhere in the novel to indicate Sterne's indebtedness, and there is even a footnote to the speech advising the reader, 'Vid. Locke' (p. 224/p. 150). Alterations to the original are minimal. What is most interesting about this particular sequence of borrowings lies in the matter rather than the manner of the use of the original. The section in *E.C.H.U.* containing the relevant passages was added to the fourth edition of 1700, which is thus the earliest edition Sterne can have been using.[6] It is only very rarely that one is able to be any more specific about the particular edition of a work from which borrowings are made for *Tristram Shandy*.

The reader who at this point feels that the passages noted earlier were atypical of Sterne's attitude to the philosopher unlike this sequence which is the one most frequently discussed by those critics anxious to establish a coherent intellectual and philosophical basis for the novel as a whole founded upon Locke's thought is in for a rude shock. In the next chapter but one following this discussion of ideas Sterne turns his attention to one of the most recurrent topics for discussion of his age: the distinction between wit and judgement. Locke's observations upon this topic were:

> For *Wit* lying most in the assemblage of *Ideas*, and putting those together with quickness and variety, wherein can be found any resemblance or congruity, thereby to make up pleasant Pictures, and agreeable Visions in the Fancy: *Judgment*, on the contrary, lies quite on the other side, in separating carefully, one from another, *Ideas*, wherein can be found the least difference, thereby to avoid being misled by Similitude, and by affinity to take one thing for another. (II, xi, §2, 156)

This passage had wide circulation in the eighteenth century, being cited by Addison in the *Spectator* No. 62 of 11 May 1711, and of all the passages utilized by Sterne is the one most likely to have been known in detail by an appreciable number of his readers. And what does he do with it?

> How is it possible there should? for that wit and judgment in this world never go together; inasmuch as they are two operations differing from each other as wide as east is from

west.—So, says *Locke*,—so are farting and hickuping say I. (p. 227/p. 153)

These are hardly the words or tone of a committed disciple.

In the passage relating to obscurity in ideas discussed above it was clear that one essential element in Sterne's comic technique was that of specificating a general idea in his original. The same device is evident in his use of Locke's *Two Treatises of Government* in Volume 3, Chapter 34. This sequence of borrowings is interesting on a number of counts: Sterne sandwiches a borrowing from Chambers' *Cyclopaedia* between two passages from Locke, and Locke's ordering of his material has been reversed, a variation seen on a number of other occasions in *Tristram Shandy*. Locke's argument is:

> He that is nourished by the Acorns he pickt up under an Oak, or the Apples he gathered from the Trees in the Wood, has certainly appropriated them to himself. No Body can deny but that the nourishment is his. I ask then, When did they begin to be his? When he digested? Or when he eat? Or when he boiled? Or when he brought them home? Or when he pickt them up? And 'tis plain, if the first gathering made them not his, nothing else could. That *labour* put a distinction between them and common.[7]

Sterne alludes to Locke as '*Didius* the great civilian', then develops the list of rhetorical questions culminating in a sudden breaking off which, like the aposiopetic conclusions to *Sentimental Journey* and Uncle Toby's suggestion of the reason for Mrs. Shandy's disinclination to be attended by Dr. Slop, allows the reader to indulge in that 'irresponsible (and nasty) trifling' in his own mind which so disturbed F. R. Leavis[8]:

> I am aware, that *Didius* the great civilian, will contest this point; and cry out against me, Whence comes this man's right to this apple? *ex confesso*, he will say,—things were in a state of nature.—The apple, as much *Frank*'s apple, as *John*'s. Pray, Mr. *Shandy*, what patent has he to shew for it? and how did it begin to be his? was it, when he set his heart upon it? or when he gather'd it? or when he chew'd it? or when he roasted it? or when he peel'd it? or when he brought it home? or when he digested?— or when he—— ——?—. (p. 263/p. 176)

After the interpolation derived from Chambers Sterne returns to Locke and after further utilization and development of

Locke's ideas concludes, 'in other words, the apple is *John's* apple' (p. 264/p. 177). The contrast between the circumlocution of the argument and the starkness of the conclusion suggests a mocking of those 'great civilians', including Locke, who devote their time to extensive discussions of the essentially obvious.

The last verbal borrowing from Locke which has been noted to date occurs towards the end of Volume 3 and once again Sterne is careful to ensure that the reader knows that the source is Locke, who had argued:

> Though the deducing one Proposition from another, or making *Inferences in Words*, be a great part of Reason, and that which it is usually employ'd about: yet the principal Act of Ratiocination is the finding the Agreement, or Disagreement of two *Ideas* one with another, by the intervention of a third. As a Man, by a Yard, finds two Houses to be of the same length, which could not be brought together to measure their Equality by *juxta*-position. (IV, xvii, § 18, 685)

This becomes:

> The gift of doing it as it should be, amongst us,—or the great and principal act of ratiocination in man, as logicians tell us, is the finding out the agreement or disagreement of two ideas one with another, by the intervention of a third; (called the *medius terminus*) just as a man, as *Locke* well observes, by a yard, finds two mens nine-pin-alleys to be of the same length, which could not be brought together, to measure their equality, by *juxta-position*. (pp. 280–81/p. 189)

This final example contains a number of elements already noticed. To what does the first 'it' in this passage refer? '*Locke* well observes' is reminiscent of the 'sagacious *Locke*', another occasion upon which initial compliment in retrospect became rather doubtful. And there is a simple but very effective alteration to the words: 'Houses' becomes 'nine-pin-alleys'. To the reader who has not read Locke, and who relies upon Sterne's references as gospel, it will appear from the ludicrous nature of the simile an example of scholarly bathos well worth citing. To the reader who is conversant with Locke's works not only will the passage have a ludicrous quality in itself, but the realization of the precise nature of the alteration will add a further dimension. Whereas the 'unlearned reader' will be able to appreciate that Locke is being pilloried, he will fail to recognize the unfairness of Sterne's action.

There are a large number of borrowings in *Tristram Shandy*; Locke is merely one of over sixty authors whose works and words were used. The intention of this essay has been to show that there is an interesting and valid alternative to the consideration of Sterne's conceptual indebtedness to Locke. The most recent full-length study of Sterne's borrowings was Ferriar's *Illustrations of Sterne* published in 1812.[9] It remains essential reading for any study of *Tristram Shandy*.

NOTES

1. Richard Davies, W. G. Day and Melvyn New (eds.), *Tristram Shandy: The Notes*, Volume III of the Florida Edition of the works of Laurence Sterne (Gainesville: University Presses of Florida), to be published in the second half of 1984.

2. See Lodwick Hartley, *Laurence Sterne in the Twentieth Century* (Chapel Hill: University of North Carolina Press, 1966), and *Laurence Sterne, An Annotated Bibliography*, 1965–77 (Boston: G. K. Hall & Co., 1978), *passim* (e.g. *s.v.* Fluchère, MacLean, Maskell, Moglen, Traugott and Tuveson), and Peter M. Briggs, 'Locke's *Essay* and the Strategies of Eighteenth-Century Satire', *Studies in Eighteenth-Century Culture* 10 (1981), 135–51.

3. Lansing Van der Heyden Hammond, *Laurence Sterne's Sermons of Mr. Yorick* (New Haven: Yale University Press, 1948), pp. 138–41.

4. William van Mildert (ed.), *The Works of the Rev. Daniel Waterland, D.D.*, 2nd edn. (Oxford, 1843), IV, 409.

5. John Locke, *E.C.H.U.*, Bk. 2, Ch. 33, §9, p. 397. Nidditch takes the fourth edition of 1700 as his copy text and this is the earliest edition Sterne could have been using; this passage is the key, being taken from the discussion of the theory of the association of ideas which first appeared in the fourth edition. This is Sterne's first overt reference to Locke. Kenneth Monkman, to whom I am indebted for reading and commenting upon a draft of this essay, has pointed out to me that there is a covert allusion in Sterne's opening chapter, which is also to Locke's 'Of the Association of Ideas'.

6. *Tristram Shandy*, pp. 224–25/pp. 150–51, derived from *E.C.H.U.*, II, xiv, §3, 181–82; §19, 188; and §9, 184.

7. John Locke, *Two Treatises of Government*, ed. Peter Laslett, 2nd edn. (Cambridge: Cambridge University Press, 1970), p. 306.

8. F. R. Leavis, *The Great Tradition* (London: Chatto & Windus, 1948), p. 2, n. 2.

'Tristram Shandy': Locke May Not Be the Key

9. On 21 January 1791 Dr. John Ferriar read to the Literary and Philosophical Society of Manchester a paper entitled 'Comments on STERNE', a paper subsequently printed in the *Memoirs* of the Society, IV, Pt. 1, (1793), 45–86, and reprinted in *The Annual Register* for 1793 (London, [1798]), pp. 379–98. This essay was considerably expanded, though in the process one or two particularly perceptive observations were omitted, and published as *Illustrations of Sterne* (London, 1798) of which a considerably revised second edition appeared in two volumes in 1812 with a rather different moral tone adopted towards the matter of the borrowings. See Alan B. Howes, *Yorick and the Critics* (New Haven: Yale University Press, 1958), pp. 81–8.

6

Against the Spleen

by ROY PORTER

1

The age of the Enlightenment was a melting-pot, a time of dissolution, criticism and regrouping in letters, humanities and science. Old verities were questioned. Aspirations to absolute certainty—the revealed Word, *a priori* rationalism, the rules of Art, direct empirical observation—were being frustrated or challenged, or were blowing up in people's faces. More sceptical and probabilistic attitudes were called for, yet this scepticism was tempered with optimism. In the ferment of ideas, experiment, endeavour, the probable, the incomplete, the subjective were winning acceptance as the realistic substitutes for the traditional but now unattainable goals of Truth or Authority, Revelation or System.

In letters, writers were experimenting with new forms (notably the novel), exploring the interplay of author, writing and audience—as *Tristram Shandy* bears abundant witness.[1] In moral philosophy, epistemology and psychology, rationalism was under a cloud; Enlightenment thinkers like Diderot (Sterne's friend)[2] and Hume (his acquaintance and admirer),[3] aware of the emptiness of prescription without description, were digging down to the foundations—in nature and culture—of consciousness, and their relations to the physiological dimension of sensations and sentiment, rooted in the organization of the nervous system. The imperative of naturalism was eliding ethics into subjectivity, energy and individuality, in ways with which we are familiar from reading Sterne.[4]

And, perhaps above all (certainly underpinning all), the scientific foundations were shifting. The Newtonian universe was accepted—orderly, regular, stable, governed by laws. But once established, it needed to be further developed. Speculation increasingly turned its attention to the outstanding riddles of the living world, to the more delicate, intractable, fluid issues of organic change, of stimulus and response, growth and generation, all viewed increasingly against a backdrop of time. As James Rodgers in particular has emphasized, life itself became a focus, a problem, a fascination.[5] What was the nature of life force? What were the vital properties? Mid-century speculative naturalists such as Diderot were pointing towards a vision of animate nature which was, at one and the same time, more 'materialistic' yet also, paradoxically, more 'vitalistic': activity and life were not the gift of external 'Creation', but intrinsic to Nature. Mid-century images of Nature conjured up a dynamic world of organized fluidity—even flux, full of striving, development, even 'evolution' of a kind, darkly linked up with an inchoate pansexuality. The wriggling homunculus would, after all, have its day.[6]

And this is, of course, the milieu of *Tristram Shandy*. The frustration of the characters is pathetic; their hobbyhorsicalism absurd, their intellectualism pompous.[7] They appear in morbid and monstrous guise: they resist nature. Ill-starred, ill-matched, they live under a pall of illness, ill-fortune and death[8] (how could that not be in a novel contemporaneous with *Rasselas* and *Candide*?). Even the name Tristram is of course connected, by an association of ideas, with the Latin '*tristus*', meaning sad. At least since Aristotle the phrase misquoted in *Tristram Shandy* as *omne animal post coitum est triste* had been current (Vol. 5, Ch. 36, p. 475/p. 317). Ironically for Tristram, it was after his *parents'* coition that he was sad.

Yet Sterne's hero and, seen through him, the rest of the cast, pulsate with an inner animation and individuality; exuberant, resilient, their vital spring is their saving grace. 'The desire of life and health is implanted in man's nature', asserts Tristram, with a touching optimism, in what could be a text for the novel. That desire encompasses Widow Wadman, carnal, concupiscent, charged with 'love-militancy'; and Walter, a learned blockhead, full of *libido disputandi*, passionate in his denial of the passions (weren't 'appetites . . . diseases?' (Vol. 5, Ch. 3, p. 424/p. 285)), indomitably questing the grail of life (' "O blessed health!" cried my father, "thou art above all gold and treasure" ' (Vol. 5, Ch. 33, p. 471/p. 315)); and indeed Tristram, joker as well as jester, whose stream of consciousness is one dribbling effusion of sublimated desire ('ask my pen' he quips, 'it governs me I govern not it'). For Tristram, for Sterne, mirth was the pill to purge melancholy, a tincture to hold mortality at bay, bravely mocking 'the grave man in black', and asserting the triumph of the quick over the dead, of generation over gravity.[9] Jesting was the best medicine. As the unquenchable Sterne poured himself out in a letter to his crony Hall-Stevenson:

> . . . I have not managed my miseries like a wise man—and if God, for my consolation under them, had not poured forth the spirit of Shandeism into me, which will not suffer me to think two moments upon any grave subject, I would else, just now, lay down and die—die—.[10]

Striving to make sense of 'this fragment of life', Sterne's characters become lost in labyrinths. But he was in no doubt about the remedy, true Shandeism. How pleased he would have been to find his medicine endorsed by that other high-priest of the cure of souls by pleasure, the utilitarian Archdeacon Paley:

> *I* will tell you in what consists the *summum bonum* of human life: it consists in reading *Tristram Shandy*, in blowing with a pair of bellows into your shoes in hot weather, and roasting potatoes under the grate in cold.[11]

2

Sterne was a consumptive. His first attacks began while an undergraduate, and then worsened in the 1750s and '60s, leading to his final demise in 1768 from a combination of tuberculosis and pleurisy. Perhaps not surprisingly for a constitutional invalid, Sterne was well versed in contemporary medicine. And the medical details in the novel—not least the obstetrical accounts—mirror, and sometimes parody, the medical knowledge of the day.[12] Satire on the man-midwife was common.

Sterne's strategy in *Tristram Shandy* is to mine the covered ways, the nervous pathways between mind and body, thought and action, intention, execution and interpretation of words and things, laying bare the ego's fortifications. His goal is generous laughter, his intent comic-serious; but his orientation—playing his attention on that fabric of fibres that constitutes a man, and his paradoxical pretensions to self-knowledge—engages directly with the great issues of the age, in a down-to-earth fashion so typical of the Enlightenment in England.[13] Amongst the foremost taxing enigmas was to grasp the slithery, elusive kinship between names and things, words and reality. The seventeenth-century scientific and empirical-philosophical movement, spearheaded by Bacon, Hobbes, Locke and the Royal Society, deplored what it saw as the ingrained fetishistic personification of words, which, animated as if they were substantial entities, spread confusion and occluded understanding.[14] Urging literal definitional meanings, Hobbes argued that words rightly handled are 'wise men's counters; they do not reckon with them; but they are the money of fools.'[15] Sterne feigns allegiance to this kind of no-nonsense linguistic nominalism. Discussing noses in Slawkenbergius's tale, Tristram professes that by 'that word, I mean a Nose and nothing more or less' (Vol. 3, Ch. 31, p. 258/p. 174). Sterne's joke, however, is that no one for a moment believes him. The nose's associations have bewitched the entire town of Strasburg, from the theologians and medical faculty to the abbess of Quedlinburg.

Indeed, as Sterne well knows, nominalism notwithstanding, the language of his day exercised a peculiar influence,[16] partly on account of two important currents of linguistic transition. On the one hand, galaxies of technical terms—the arcana of chemistry, natural philosophy, metaphysical theology, medicine—hitherto relatively restricted in circulation, were being popularized and were passing into common speech with looser connotations. And at the same time, words traditionally anchored in tangible, physical and literal meanings were widening in range, taking on predominantly abstract and figurative usage. Terms such as acid, acrimony, acerbity, insipid, were becoming absorbed into the no-man's land of psychology, while retaining their basic physical implications.[17] Sterne collared the opportunities these developments afforded for a punning polysemy, bouncing physical-organic and metaphysical meanings off against each other, spotlighting how words could be scalpel-probes, revealing the secret ramifications of a man's workings, but uncovering deeper problems all the time.

Take 'gravity'. Yorick, Tristram tells us, 'had an invincible dislike and opposition in his nature to gravity', being 'mercurial and sublimated' (Vol. 1, Ch. 11, p. 27–8/p. 22), terms rooted in astrology and alchemy, whose figurative meanings were perhaps becoming detached from obsolescent literal origins. Quixotic Yorick lacks gravity, being (should one say literally?) light-headed—a scatter-brained jester:

> With all this sail, poor *Yorick* carried not one ounce of ballast; he was utterly unpractised in the world; and, at the age of twenty-six, knew just about as well how to steer his course in it, as a romping, unsuspicious girl of thirteen: So that upon his first setting out, the brisk gale of his spirits, as you will imagine, ran him foul ten times in a day of somebody's tackling. (Vol. 1, Ch. 11, pp. 27–8/p. 22)

But he also exposes gravity for being a pose, an affectation of habit: 'the very essence of gravity was design, and consequently deceit, a cloak for ignorance.' And gravity is furthermore leadenfooted dullness (classically captured in Pope's *Peri Bathous*, the art of sinking); it is Saturnine melancholy[18]; it is Newton's clockwork universe; and it is, above all, the grave. Yorick jingles his bells at all of them, especially at Death.

The satire against gravity is kept up.

> Now your graver gentry having little or no kind of chance in aiming at the one,—unless they laid hold of the other,—pray what do you think would become of them?—Why, Sirs, in spight of all their *gravities*, they must e'en have been contented to have gone with their insides naked: . . . (Vol. 3, Ch. 20, p. 237/p. 160)

It is worth noting that various natural philosophers of the eighteenth century such as the Scot James Hutton saw gravity as symbolically the power of 'death' in the universe, countered

by heat as the principle of life.[19] Walter Shandy similarly is
only too well aware of the occult powers of words. He comes
clean on the magic of names. We may mock and snigger; but
as Walter ripostes, 'your BILLY, Sir! Would you, for the
world, have called him JUDAS?' (Vol. 1, Ch. 19, pp. 58–9/
p. 44). He keeps Ernulphus's dire curse against the body
handy on his parlour shelf, for emergency use. All this is of
course ludicrous—partly because it backfires. After all, Dr.
Slop gives Obadiah the full works of Ernulphus's anathema:

> "May he (*Obadiah*) be cursed in all the faculties of his body! . . .
> and in his groin," (God in heaven forbid, quoth my uncle
> *Toby*)—"in his thighs, in his genitals," (my father shook his
> head) "and in his hips, and in his knees, his legs, and feet, and
> toe-nails. . . ." (Vol. 3, Ch. 11, p. 209/p. 141)

Yet—cursed genitals and all—it is only the coachman
Obadiah who seems capable of procreating. Though, despite
Widow Wadman's suspicions, and endless innuendo, Toby is
probably not intended by Sterne to be physically impotent: the
joke here is that Toby's impotence is seated in the *head*.[20]
Sterne's ironic point, of course, is that while Dr. Slop and
Walter Shandy (who was 'given to close reason upon
the smallest matters' (Vol. 1, Ch. 3, p. 4/p. 7)) pursue great
learning, they are both oblivious of reality, possessed by their
own pet medical theories, canting about '*consubstantials*,
impriments and *occludents*' (Vol. 5, Ch. 40, p. 482/p. 321)—('you
puzzle me to death', bewails Uncle Toby, on the receiving end
of one of Walter's lectures (Vol. 3, Ch. 18, p. 224/p. 151)).

Recent structuralist and deconstructionist criticism has
probed the punning elisions between the acts of writing, living,
creating and dying, getting and spending.[21] Sterne, eliding the
pen and the penis, juggles these possibilities ceaselessly,
hinting at the unconscious springs of action from the evacuating
Diego in Slawkenbergius's tale who 'eased his mind against
the wall' (Vol. 4, p. 322/p. 215), through to the auto-erotic
ecstasies of the author:

> Bless us!—what noble work we should make!—how should I
> tickle it off!—and what spirits should I find myself in, to be
> writing away for such readers!—and you—just heaven! . . .
> —'tis too much,—I am sick,—I faint away deliciously at the

thoughts of it!—'tis more than nature can bear!—lay hold of me,—I am giddy,—I am stone blind,—I'm dying,—I am gone.—Help! Help! Help!—But hold,——I grow something better again.[22] (p. 229/p. 154)

But there is—as the above quotation suggests—a personal *idée fixe* for Sterne: preoccupation with the relations of writing with health. At one stage Toby's life was 'put in jeopardy by words' (Vol. 2, Ch. 2, p. 101/p. 71), and writing can be terminal ('my OPINIONS will be the death of me', puns Tristram (Vol. 4, Ch. 13, p. 342/p. 228)—after all, his book is meant to be his *life* and opinions, yet he will spend all his life writing them. And writing proves so often to be diseased. In his *Sentimental Journey* Sterne diagnoses Smollett's book of travels as a secretion of spleen and gall, and banters:

> —I'll tell it, cried Smelfungus [Smollett], to the world. You had better tell it, said I, to your physician.

Yet for Tristram, as surely for Sterne, and Rabelais and Burton before, writing is also par excellence *therapy*, drawing pain's sting: 'If 'tis wrote against any thing,—'tis wrote, an' please your worships, against the spleen'[24] (Vol. 4, Ch. 22, p. 360/p. 239); for Shandeism is a medicine, tonic for health:

> And now that you have just got to the end of these four volumes—the thing I have to *ask* is, how you feel your heads? my own akes dismally—as for your healths, I know, they are much better—True *Shandeism*, think what you will against it, opens the heart and lungs, and like all those affections which partake of its nature, it forces the blood and other vital fluids of the body to run freely thro' its channels, and makes the wheel of life run long and chearfully round. (Vol. 4, Ch. 32, p. 401/ p. 270)

—a view parodied with ludicrous panache when Yorick prescribes the 'herbal' remedy for Phutatorius's member, frazzled by the roast chestnut, which is the therapy of the word, the printing cure through the application of a fresh leaf of Phutatorius's new book, hot from the press.

Ludicrous, some would say, because what else was left for the likes of Sterne in a heartless world, than to humiliate man, to make the homunculus the prey of a cruel sport? For an influential tradition amongst literary criticism and the history of ideas, culture and science has averred that the Scientific Revolution, and the Cartesian mind-body dualism which backed the mechanical world-view, were spiritual disasters in that they atomized and dissected what had been a unified, rich, holistic culture, in which man was in organical touch with nature, spirit, soul and feelings.[25] In its place science imposed something sterilized and lifeless, a meaningless mechanical system which divided and ruled through an array of dehumanizing dualisms: man divorced from nature, mind from matter, body from soul, reason from feeling, fact from value. Sensibilities were dissociated, selves divided, nature disenchanted. Confined in such an absurd, and maddening intellectual straitjacket, what could a poor brain-child of a Cartesian world like Tristram do but intellectualize his own alienation, what could Sterne do but libel his robot creations?[26]

There is obviously a grain of truth in this; Sterne makes merry at the preposterous high-rise speculations of broad rationalists, reductionists and mechanists, wilfully blind to the chasms between their theory and reality (though a glance at Rabelais's or Erasmus's wars against inanities shows that arid *esprit de système* was no monopoly of the post-Cartesian world). But the critique is generally off-beam. For most scholars nowadays would question whether the 'New Science' and mechanical philosophy were really Trojan horses, admitting disastrous self-alienating dichotomies.[27] Within the fields of medicine and the life-sciences, for example, mechanistic dualism—far more subtle in any case than knock-about denunciations of it would allow[28]—did not carry the day. Rather, the classical framework, heavily indebted to Hippocrates, Aristotle and Galen, retained great vitality, and traditional medical categories, such as ideas of the humours, non-naturals, and the vital and animal spirits, complexions and temperaments, remained integral. Sterne's exploration of the dialectical reciprocity of body and mind is comic—it is meant to be; but it is funny not because it was a deliberately quaint revamping of what had become archaisms, or a shaft against entrenched mechanistic orthodoxy. A glimpse of Sterne's own personal trials, griefs and joys, his self-absorbed responses to the temperature of his health expressed in private correspondence, bears this out. His consciousness and body were tinglingly in touch with each other, his feelings—of love, expectancy, despair—registering themselves bodily, in fevers, heartache, trembling, recovery. He never doubted illness could stem from 'affliction of' the 'mind',[29] and charted how somatic ills enacted the troughs and peaks of his spirit. 'Worn out with fevers of all kinds', he wrote to Eliza,

> but most, by that fever of the heart with which I'm eternally wasting, and shall waste till I see Eliza again: dreadful Suffering of 15 months! It may be more.[30]

Sterne's letters to Eliza constantly play on the theme of love as both illness and medicine. Sterne enjoys mocking medicine. But—like Defoe, Fielding, Smollett and other contemporary novelists[31]—Sterne automatically deployed the concepts and vocabulary of traditional medicine in sketching character and social behaviour. Walter Shandy, for example, was a classic medical 'type', a man of choleric humour.[32] In behaviour, he is prone to sudden fits of temper; he fumes, splutters and frets, going off 'like gunpowder' (Vol. 3, Ch. 41, p. 283/p. 191). Physiologically he is full of 'heat' (choler is hot and dry). Diagnostically he is apoplectic: there is often 'a prodigious suffusion of blood in my father's countenance' ('all the blood in his body seemed to rush up into his face' (Vol. 3, Ch. 5, p. 191/p. 128)). Sterne is also psychologically accurate: true to the choleric type, Walter has a strong wit (full of hot air), but scant judgement—'his rhetoric and conduct were at perpetual handy-cuffs' (Vol. 3, Ch. 21, p. 239/p. 161). And being intellectual in bent, Walter knows he has a 'subacid humour', and follows the recommended medical counter-régime, holding off liquor, sticking to water, and lying down when he explodes—horizontality, Tristram notes, is the optimal position for bearing pain '(and for aught I know, pleasure too)'.

Uncle Toby, by contrast (who took his character 'more from blood than either wind or water', i.e., more from heredity than environment),[33] is 'sanguine' in temperament, a mix of hot and moist elements. True to type, he is disposed to bear affliction (all the four years his wound is healing, he is patience and courtesy personified), yet is duller in his wits (his brain is like a 'smoke-jack'). Moreover, his recovery is a text-book case of psycho-therapeutics.[34] As any expert physician would have recommended, to ward off the melancholy which enforced idleness supposedly entailed, he took up a 'hobby-horse' ('great relief' as occupational therapy, according to the most acclaimed 'nervous' doctor of the age, George Cheyne, an author Sterne certainly read). In *The English malady* (1733), one of the most widely read discussions of melancholy of the period, Cheyne writes that he 'would earnestly recommend to all those afflicted with Nervous Distempers, always to have some innocent entertaining Amusement to employ themselves in'. 'Without such a help', he adds, it was 'absolutely impossible to keep the Mind easy, and prevent its wearing out the Body, as the Sword does the Scabbard'. What the amusement was made no difference, 'provided it be but a *Hobby-Horse* . . . and stop the Current of Reflexion and intense Thinking, which Persons of weak Nerves are apt to run into'. Occupation as therapy was of course deeply traditional wisdom for melancholy, found, for example, in Burton, to whom Sterne was deeply indebted.[35] Yet Toby's hobby-horse almost gallops away with him, threatening to become an obsession, a ruling passion. Single-minded pre-occupations, medicine taught, led to madness, and one modern commentator, M. V. DePorte, has argued that Sterne meant to depict Toby as becoming what contemporaries would have recognized as mad.[36]

Tristram, for his part, behaves as one would expect from a man whose loss of animal spirits is complicated by consumption. His complaints combine to make him light-headed, feverish, impetuous. He is all fits and starts, prey to sudden sallies, whimsical, prattling. He has his father's keen wit, but lacks concentration,[37] being all digression. On account of his consumption, his humours are all jumbled together, his feelings delicate and close to the surface, brimful of sentiment.[38] His antennae acutely conscious of the register of his emotional inflexions:

> I enter upon this part of my story in the most pensive and melancholy frame of mind, that ever sympathetic breast was touched with.—My nerves relax as I tell it.—Every line I write, I feel an abatement of the quickness of my pulse, and of that careless alacrity with it, which every day of my life prompts me to say and write a thousand things I should not.—And this

moment that I last dipp'd my pen into my ink, I could not help taking notice what a cautious air of sad composure and solemnity there appear'd in my manner of doing it.—Lord! how different from the rash jerks, and hare-brain'd squirts thou art wont, *Tristram!* to transact it with in other humours, . . . (Vol. 3, Ch. 28, p. 254/p. 171)

(a self-portrait ratified by the Sterne we observe in the *Sentimental Journey* and the *Journal to Eliza*).

For Sterne, medicine was not an alien world of incomprehensible theories and dehumanizing scientific models of man (though that didn't stop him from poking fun at learned idiocy). Rather, it provided him with the language, the medium, through which he sought to understand his own, and the human, condition. As such it was good therapy indeed, 'against the spleen'.

NOTES

1. For an introduction to the vast literature see W. Park, '*Tristram Shandy* and the New "Novel of Sensibility" ', *Studies in the Novel*, VI (1974), 268–79.

2. A. G. Fredman, *Diderot and Sterne* (New York: Octagon Books, 1973).

3. F. Doherty, 'Sterne and Hume: A Bicentenary Essay', *Essays and Studies*, XXII (1969), 71–87.

4. See, among a vast literature on the psycho-physiology of 'feeling', L. Bredvold, *The Natural History of Sensibility* (Detroit: Wayne State University Press); S. Moravia, 'The Enlightenment and the Sciences of Man', *History of Science*, XVIII (1980), 247–68; K. Figlio, 'Theories of Perception and the Physiology of Mind in the Late Eighteenth Century', *History of Science*, XIII (1975), 177–212. A dim view of the descent into chaotic subjectivity is taken by L. Crocker in his *An Age of Crisis: Man and World in Eighteenth Century French Thought* (Baltimore: Johns Hopkins University Press, 1959).

5. For mid-eighteenth century rejection of mechanism in the life and human sciences, and the quest for a unifying science which would be more satisfactorily materialistic and monistic, yet also do justice to the categories of life, vitality, process, energy, and sensitivity, see A. O. Lovejoy, *The Great Chain of Being* (Cambridge, Mass.: Harvard University Press, 1936), Ch. 8; T. S. Hall, *A History of General Physiology* (Chicago: University of Chicago Press, 1969); F. Duchesneau, *La Physiologie des Lumières* (The Hague: Martinus Nijhoff, 1982); J. Roger, *Les Sciences de la Vie dans la Pensée Française du XVIIIᵉ siècle* (Paris: Colin,

Against the Spleen

1971); *idem*, 'The Living World', in G. S. Rousseau and Roy Porter (eds.), *The Ferment of Knowledge* (Cambridge: Cambridge University Press, 1980), pp. 253–83; C. Kiernan, *Science and Enlightenment in Eighteenth Century France* (Geneva: Voltaire Foundation, 1968); T. Brown, 'From Mechanism to Vitalism in Eighteenth Century English Physiology', *Journal of the History of Biology*, VII (1974), 179–216; R. French, *Robert Whytt, The Soul and Medicine* (London: Wellcome Institute, 1969); P. M. Heimann and J. E. McGuire, 'Newtonian Forces and Lockean Powers: Concepts of Matter in Eighteenth Century Thought', *Historical Studies in the Physical Sciences*, III (1971), 233–306; H. W. Piper, *The Active Universe* (London: Athlone Press, 1962); E. Sewell, *The Orphic Voice* (London: Routledge and Kegan Paul, 1961); L. Crocker, 'Diderot and Eighteenth Century Transformism', in B. Glass, O. Temkin and W. Straus (eds.), *Forerunners of Darwin* (Baltimore: Johns Hopkins University Press, 1959), pp. 114–43. All these developments are valuably digested in relation to Sterne in J. Rodgers, 'Ideas of Life in *Tristram Shandy*' (Ph.D. thesis, University of East Anglia, 1978).

6. For the Enlightenment's libido-liberating claim that the erotic is the healthy see J. Hagstrum, *Sex and Sensibility: Ideal and Erotic Love from Milton to Mozart* (London: University of Chicago Press, 1980); Roy Porter, 'Mixed Feelings: The Enlightenment and Sexuality in Britain', in P.-G. Boucé (ed.), *Sexuality in Eighteenth Century Britain* (Manchester: Manchester University Press, 1982), pp. 1–27; *idem*, 'The Sexual Politics of James Graham', *The British Journal of Eighteenth Century Studies*, V (1982), 199–205; P.-G. Boucé, 'Some Sexual Beliefs and Myths in Eighteenth Century Britain', in Boucé (ed.) listed above, pp. 28–47.

7. For Sterne and the satire upon learning see M. New, *Laurence Sterne as Satirist* (Gainesville: University of Florida Press, 1969); D. W. Jefferson, '*Tristram Shandy* and its Tradition', in B. Ford (ed.), *The Pelican Guide to English Literature*, IV (Harmondsworth: Pelican Books, 1957), pp. 335–45; *idem*, 'Tristram Shandy and the Tradition of Learned Wit', *Essays in Criticism*, I (1951), 225–48; J. Traugott, *Tristram Shandy's World: Sterne's Philosophical Rhetoric* (Berkeley: University of California Press, 1954); W. Watson, 'Sterne's Satire on Mechanism: A Study of *Tristram Shandy*' (Ph.D. Diss., University of Toronto, 1951). Sterne's 'Rabelaisianism' can be readily seen from M. Screech, *Rabelais* (London: Duckworth, 1979).

8. For contemporary attitudes towards death see J. McManners, *Death and the Enlightenment* (Oxford: Oxford University Press, 1981); P. Ariès, *The Hour of our Death* (Harmondsworth: Allen Lane, 1981).

9. M. V. DePorte, *Nightmares and Hobby-horses* (San Marino, Cal.: Huntingdon Library, 1974), pp. 125f; L. J. Rather, 'Old and New Views of the Emotions and Bodily Changes', *Clio Medica*, I (1965), 1–25; T. H. Jobe, 'Medical Theories of Melancholia in the Seventeenth and Early Eighteenth Centuries', *Clio Medica*, XI (1976), 217–31; Esther Fischer-Homberger, *Hypochondrie, Melancholie bis Neurose: Krankheiten und Zustandbilden* (Bern: Hans Huber, 1970).

10. *Letters*, p. 139.

95

11. H. Digby Beste, *Personal and Literary Memorials* (London: Henry Colburn, 1829), p. 209. I owe this quotation to Michael Neve.
12. For discussion and documentation see D. Furst, 'Sterne and Physick: Images of Health and Disease in *Tristram Shandy*' (Ph.D. Diss., Columbia University, 1974); L. S. King, *The Medical World of the Eighteenth Century* (Chicago: University of Chicago Press, 1958). For Sterne's medical learning see A. Cash, 'The Birth of Tristram Shandy: Sterne and Dr. Burton', in P.-G. Boucé (ed.) *Sexuality in Eighteenth Century Britain* (Manchester: Manchester University Press, 1982), pp. 198–224; L. Landa, 'The Shandean Homunculus: The Background of Sterne's "Little Gentleman" ', in C. Camden (ed.), *Restoration and Eighteenth Century Literature: Essays in Honour of Alan Dugald McKillop* (Chicago: University of Chicago Press, 1963), pp. 49–68; and for a general survey on the interface of medicine and literature G. S. Rousseau, 'Science and Literature, the state of the art', *Isis*, LXIX (1978), 583–91; *idem*, 'Literature and Medicine: the State of the Field', *Isis*, LXXII (1981), 406–24.

For Sterne's obstetrical ideas and their background see A. Dorna, 'Burton (Dr. Slop): His Forceps and his Foes', *Journal of Obstetrics and Gynaecology of the British Empire*, XXIII (1913), 3–24, 65–86; W. Radcliffe, 'Dr. John Burton and his Whimsical Contrivance', *Medical Bookman and Historian*, II (1948), 349–55; R. Davies, 'A Memoir of John Burton', *Yorkshire Antiquarian Journal*, II (1877–78), 403–40; J. Donison, *Midwives and Medical Men: A History of Inter-Professional Rivalries and Women's Rights* (New York: Schocken, 1977); E. Shorter, *A History of Women's Bodies* (Harmondsworth: Allen Lane, 1983); B. This, *La Requête des Enfants à Naître* (Paris: Seuil, 1982); R. W. Johnstone, *William Smellie, the Master of British Midwifery* (Edinburgh: E. and S. Livingstone, 1952); J. Glaister, *Dr. William Smellie and his Contemporaries* (Glasgow: J. Maclehose, 1894); H. R. Spencer, *The History of British Midwifery from 1650 to 1800* (London: Bale & Danielsson, 1927). Note the poignant personal element: how Sterne would have wished to have a son survive childbirth!
13. Roy Porter, 'The Enlightenment in England', in Roy Porter and Mikuláš Teich (eds.), *The Enlightenment in National Context* (Cambridge: Cambridge University Press, 1981), pp. 1–18.
14. R. F. Jones, *Ancients and Moderns* (St. Louis: Washington University Press, 1936); B. J. Shapiro, *Probability and Certainty in Seventeenth Century England* (Princeton: Princeton University Press, 1983); A. C. Howell, 'Res et Verba: Words and Things', *E.L.H.*, XIII (1946), 131–42.
15. T. Hobbes, *Leviathan*, ed. C. B. MacPherson (Harmondsworth: Pelican Books, 1968), p. 106.
16. See D. Davie, *The Language of Science and the Language of Literature 1700–1740* (London: Sheed and Ward, 1963); J. Arthos, *The Language of Natural Description in Eighteenth Century Poetry* (Ann Arbor: University of Michigan Press, 1949); W. K. Wimsatt, *Philosophical Words* (New Haven: Yale University Press, 1948); S. Tucker, *Protean Shape* (London: Athlone Press, 1967).

Against the Spleen

17. For some of these mutations see Roy Porter, 'The Doctor and the Word', *Medical Sociology News*, IX (1983), 21–8.
18. R. Klibansky, *Saturn and Melancholy* (London: Nelson, 1964).
19. See Roy Porter, *The Making of Geology* (Cambridge: Cambridge University Press, 1977), p. 190f.
20. See M. Sinfield, 'Uncle Toby's Potency: Some Critical and Authorial Confusions in *Tristram Shandy*', *Notes and Queries*, 223 (1978), 54–55.
21. A chronologically relevant example is T. Eagleton, *The Rape of Clarissa* (Oxford: Basil Blackwell, 1982). See also R. Barthes, *Le Plaisir du Texte* (Paris: Seuil, 1973); T. Eagleton, *Literary Theory* (Oxford: Basil Blackwell, 1983); J. Culler, *On Deconstruction* (London: Routledge and Kegan Paul, 1983).
22. Sterne's hinting at the unconscious springs of action, and its parallels to the psychology of the nerves of Robert Whytt, is excellently discussed in J. Rodgers's 'Ideas of life in *Tristram Shandy*'. See also L. L. Whyte, *The Unconscious before Freud* (London: J. Friedmann, 1960).
23. *SJ*, p. 118.
24. For the spleen—both an abdominal organ and a fashionable term for melancholy—see C. Moore, *Backgrounds of English Literature 1700–1760* (Minneapolis: Illinois University Press, 1953); O. Doughty, 'The English Malady of the Eighteenth Century', *Review of English Studies*, II (1926), 257–69; E. Fischer-Homberger, 'Hypochondriasis of the Eighteenth Century—Neurosis of the Present Century?', *Bulletin of the History of Medicine*, XLVI (1972), 391–401; Roy Porter, 'The Rage of Party: A Glorious Revolution in English Psychiatry?', *Medical History*, XXVII (1983), 35–50.
25. For various forms of this view see F. Bottomley, *Attitudes to the Body in Western Christendom* (London: Lepus, 1979); N. O. Brown, *Life Against Death* (London: Sphere, 1968); M. Berman, *The Re-enchantment of the World* (London: Cornell University Press, 1982); F. Capra, *The Turning Point: Science, Society and the Rising Culture* (New York: Simon and Schuster, 1982); D. Bush, *Science and English Poetry* (Oxford: Oxford University Press, 1950); F. Alexander, *The Medical Value of Psychoanalysis* (London: Allen & Unwin, 1932); R. Grinker, *Fifty Years in Psychiatry* (Springfield, Ill.: Charles C. Thomas, 1979).
26. For the view that Sterne essentially satirizes his characters see M. New, *Laurence Sterne as Satirist*.
27. For discussions of medical continuity, the irrelevance of the 'Cartesian' dualism, and the continuation of psychosomatic approaches to health and personality see W. F. Bynum, 'Health, Disease and Medical Care', in G. S. Rousseau and Roy Porter (eds.), *The Ferment of Knowledge* (Cambridge: Cambridge University Press, 1980), pp. 211–55; G. S. Rousseau, 'Psychology', in ibid., pp. 143–210; L. S. King, *The Medical World of the Eighteenth Century* (Chicago: University of Chicago Press, 1958); L. Rather, *Mind and Body in Eighteenth Century Medicine* (Berkeley: California University Press, 1965); Roy Porter, 'Le Prospettive della "Follia": Scienza, Medicina e Letteratura nell'Inghilterra del 1700', *Intersezioni*, II (1982), 55–76.

28. R. B. Carter, *Descartes' Medical Philosophy* (Baltimore: Johns Hopkins University Press, 1983), demonstrates the extent of Descartes' own explorations of psychosomatic interplay: see, for example, pp. 113–14.
29. *Letters*, p. 318.
30. Ibid., p. 323.
31. For traditional medical categories in eighteenth-century novels see R. Stephanson, 'Defoe's "Malade Imaginaire"': The Historical Foundations of Mental Illness in *Roxana*', *Huntingdon Library Quarterly*, XLV (1982), 100–18; R. Erickson, 'Moll's Fate, "Mother Midnight" and *Moll Flanders*', *Studies in Philology*, LXXVI (1979), 75–100; G. S. Rousseau, *Tobias Smollett: Essays of Two Decades* (Edinburgh: T. T. Clark, 1982). For satirical play with such ideas see M. V. DePorte, 'Digressions and madness in *A Tale of a Tub* and *Tristram Shandy*', *Huntingdon Library Quarterly*, XXXIV (1970), 43–57; R. Paulson, *Theme and Structure in Swift's Tale of a Tub* (New Haven: Yale University Press, 1960); J. R. Clark, *Form and Frenzy in Swift's Tale of a Tub* (Ithaca: Cornell University Press, 1970); D. B. Morris, 'The Kinship of Madness in Pope's *Dunciad*', *Philological Quarterly*, L (1972), 813–31; G. Rosen, 'Forms of Irrationality in the Eighteenth Century', in H. E. Pagliaro (ed.), *Irrationality in Eighteenth Century Culture* (Cleveland, Ohio: Case Western Reserve University Press, 1972), pp. 255–88.
32. For Sterne's humoral characterization and its medical sources see D. C. Furst, 'Sterne and Physick'.
33. For medical environmentalism see F. K. Stanzel, '*Tristram Shandy* und die Klimattheorie', *Germanisch-Romanische Monatsschrift*, XXI (1971), 16–28; L. J. Jordanova, 'Earth Science and Environmental Medicine: The Synthesis of the Late Enlightenment', in L. J. Jordanova and Roy Porter (eds.), *Images of the Earth* (Chalfont St. Giles, Bucks.: British Society for the History of Science, 1979), pp. 119–46.
34. This is well discussed in DePorte, *Nightmares and Hobby-horses*, p. 147.
35. H. J. Jackson, 'Sterne, Burton and Ferriar: Allusion to the *Anatomy of Melancholy* in volumes five to nine of *Tristram Shandy*', *Philological Quarterly*, LIV (1975), 457–70.
36. M. V. DePorte, 'Digressions and madness in *A Tale of a Tub* and *Tristram Shandy*', *Huntingdon Library Quarterly*, XXXIV (1970), 43–57.
37. For a grave verdict on Tristram's infantile character see P. M. Spacks, *Imagining a Self* (Cambridge, Mass.: Harvard University Press, 1976).
38. For the sentimental see Erik Erametsa, *A Study of the Word 'Sentimental' and of Eighteenth Century Sentimentalism in England* (Helsinki, 1951); R. S. Crane, 'Suggestions Towards a Genealogy of the Man of Feeling', *E.L.H.*, I (1934), 205–30; G. S. Rousseau, 'Nerves, Spirits and Fibres: Towards defining the Origins of Sensibility—with a Postscript 1976', *The Blue Guitar* (Rome, 1976), II, 125–53; K. MacLean, 'Imagination and Sympathy: Sterne and Adam Smith', *Journal of the History of Ideas*, X (1949), 399–410.
39. Though Tristram is not simply Sterne. See O. P. James, *The Relation of 'Tristram Shandy' to the Life of Sterne* (The Hague: Mouton, 1966).

7

Tristram and the Animal Spirits

by VALERIE GROSVENOR MYER

1

Everyone knows that Mrs. Shandy's ill-timed question to her husband, *Pray my dear, have you not forgot to wind up the clock?* (Vol. 1, Ch. 1, p. 2/p. 5), is the cause of Tristram's misfortunes. But the modern reader may well find himself puzzled. Why should the interruption have such dire effects? What has the scattering of the animal spirits to do with Tristram as a 'child of decrepitude! interruption! mistake!' (Vol. 4, Ch. 19, p. 354/p. 236)? And what, exactly, at the time of writing, were the animal spirits? This essay attempts to outline their history and their significance within the scheme of *Tristram Shandy*, drawing together materials already well-known to scholars but baffling to new readers of the book, with one or two more recondite examples.

The answers to the questions today's reader might ask relate to the interpretation of the novel. Mr. Shandy, interrupted by his wife's question in the middle of lovemaking, loses concentration and lets go: he has an involuntary emission. Why should this be disastrous? Nathaniel Highmore's *The History of Generation* (1651) supplies the answer. Highmore was a medical man, a friend of Sir William Harvey, widely known and respected. The *Dictionary of National Biography* says of him: 'Though perfectly sound in his views as regards the circulation of the blood, the physiological remarks of Highmore are sometimes medieval.'

During the preceding centuries, the problem had been much discussed: how did the human embryo acquire its soul? Some thought God acted directly, putting a soul or *anima sensibilis* into the foetus when it was formed, others thought the soul came from the father, in the sperm itself. Highmore holds the second of these medieval opinions. According to Highmore, the seed of man 'consists of two parts, Material Atomes, animated and directed by a spiritual force, proper to the species whose the seed it is. . . .'[1]

Highmore explains:

> In all involuntary emissions, the soul is not communicated to the seed. But then onely, when the generator's soul, by a voluntary act, intent on propagation and multiplying herself unto another individuum, diffuseth herself into the now parting sperm, then only is it prolifical. When coming into a convenient receptacle, where those Atomes may repose; being moved onely by that soul which accompanied them, and from which they have received their orders and commands, are soon settled into their proper places, and becomes a perfect individuum of that species.[2]

Tristram is a less than perfect individuum because his father's sperm, involuntarily emitted, is not accompanied by the directing spiritual force which should accompany it to its resting-place. The homunculus is deprived of its natural guides because his father's concentration was disturbed. The soul is feminine because the writer is thinking of Latin, *Anima*. The 'animal spirits' as we shall see, are spirits pertaining to the soul.

The account of the damage to the homunculus is less narrative than speculative:

> Now, dear Sir, what if any accident had befallen him in his way alone? Or that, thro' terror of it, natural to so young a traveller, my little gentleman had got to his journey's end miserably spent;—his muscular strength and virility worn down to a thread;—his own animal spirits ruffled beyond description,— (Vol. 1, Ch. 2, p. 3/p. 6).

Virility is not Tristram's strong point, any more than it is his father's. Tristram can only apologize to his dear Jenny for what has not happened in the bedroom (Vol. 7, Ch. 29, p. 624/p. 415). In his account of the misfortunes of the homunculus, Sterne is making play with Locke as well as with the medical theorists. In *Some Thoughts Concerning Education* we read of the harmful effects of fear on young children.

> Let not any fearful apprehensions be talked into them, nor terrible objects surprise them. This often so shatters and discomposes the spirits, that they never recover it [*sic*] again; but during their whole life, upon the first suggestion or appearance of any terrifying idea, are scattered and confounded; the body is enervated and the mind disturbed, and the man scarce himself or capable of any composed or rational action. Whether this be from an habitual motion of the *animal spirits* [my italics] introduced by the first strong impression, or from the alteration of the constitution by some more unaccountable way, this is certain, that so it is. Instances of such who in a weak timorous mind, have borne, all their lives through, the effect of a fright when they were young, are everywhere to be seen.[3]

Locke emphasizes the crucial importance of early experience. Sterne pushes Locke's idea to its theoretical limit: what about a fright at the earliest experience of all, the moment of conception? Tristram's body is enervated and his mind disturbed, as he tells us himself. Because of the involuntary emission, which results in loneliness and terror for the homunculus, Tristram grows up with spirits 'scattered and confounded', the victim of weakness and melancholy.

2

The history of the animal spirits is complicated. At the time Sterne wrote, the concept was already fading, along with the concepts of 'radical heat' and 'radical moisture'. Sterne plays with theories of body, mind and soul taken from the older writers, which the medical profession of his day was busily discarding under the impact of experimental science.

Friedrich Hoffman's *Fundamenta medicinae*, published in 1693, deals with the 'vital motion of our machine and sensation'. Hoffman writes that 'vital actions depend on the proper laudable and even motion of the fluid parts, especially the animal spirits.' When the 'vital actions . . . are injured, then disease . . . is said to be present'.[4] Hoffman's translator, Lester Snow King, comments that Hoffman's position is a synthesis, derived from Galen, combined with the new physiology and the new chemical ideas. Hoffman retained the older concept of a delicate fluid responsible for vital activity, and this 'nervous fluid' was, says King, the lineal descendant of the animal spirits.

The different kinds of spirits derive ultimately from Plato, as summarized by Cornford:

> In Plato's myth of creation (*The Timaeus*) the three parts [of the soul] are lodged in the head, the chest, and the belly and organs of generation; and the reason alone is immortal and separable from the body.[5]

Aristotle divided the soul into four faculties: the vegetative, sensitive, intellective and motive.[6] But as St. Thomas Aquinas, in his translation of and commentary on Aristotle's treatise, points out, Aristotle elsewhere includes the appetitive, and sets aside 'the usual threefold division . . . into vegetative, sensitive and intellectual'.[7] This commentary reduced the powers of the soul once more to a triad. The revived popularity of the animal spirits in the Renaissance was due, like so much else, to Ficino: in addition to soul there was a spirit, finely material, which could be intermediary between soul and body. This chimed conveniently with Galen's doctrine of the natural, vital and animal spirits, in ascending order of value: the natural or vegetal spirits, concerned with growth and nutrition, in the liver; the vital or sensitive spirits in the lungs and heart, the seat of the 'passions' or emotions; and the animal spirits, a more refined kind of vital spirit, carried by the blood to the brain. Tillyard usefully summarizes:

> The brain rules the top of man's body, and is the seat of the rational and immortal part. The animal spirits are the executive agents of the brain through the nerves and partake both of the body and of the soul.[8]

During the sixteenth century a medico-mystical tradition of writing about the spirits grew up, as they were considered 'evidence' for the immortality of the soul. Miguel Servetus (1511–53) compared the animal spirits to a ray of light.[9] The relationship between the faculties of the soul (which coincided with those of the three orders of spirits) and the corresponding parts of the human body are expressed in the diagrams illustrating the works of the hermetecist Robert Fludd.[10]

Ephraim Chambers, in his *Cyclopaedia, Or, An Universal Dictionary of Arts and Sciences*, second edition, 1738, the one Sterne probably used, defines 'spirits' as

> in medicine the most subtile and volatile part, or juice of the body; by means whereof, all the functions, and operations thereof, are supposed to be performed. . . .
>
> The ancients made a four-fold division of spirits into vital, animal, natural and genital; whereof, the first they placed at the heart; the second in the brain; the third in the stomach and liver; and the last in the testicles; but as this division is founded on a false hypothesis, it is now deservedly set aside.
>
> The moderns usually divide *spirits* into *vital* and *animal*.
>
> *Vital* SPIRITS, are only the finest, and most agitated parts of the blood: whereon its motion, heat depend. . . .
>
> *Animal* SPIRITS, are an exceedingly thin, subtile, moveable fluid juice or humour separated from the blood in the cortex of the brain, hence received into the minute fibres of the medulla, and by them discharged into the nerves, by which is conveyed through every part of the body, to be the instrument of sensation, muscular motion, &c.
>
> The *animal* spirits, called also nervous spirits and nervous juice, only differ from the vital spirits, in that these last are still mixed and blended with the grosser parts of the blood, and circulate along with it; whereas, the animal *spirits* are secreted thence by the glands whereof the cortical substance is composed; and have the motion, circulation, &c., peculiar to themselves. . . .
>
> The existence of the *animal spirits* is controverted; but the infinite use they are of in the animal oeconomy and the exceedingly lame account we should have of any of the animal functions without them, will keep the greatest part of the world on their side. And, in effect, the learned Boerhaave has gone a good way towards a demonstration of their reality.

Chambers summarizes Boerhaave's theory, which is physiological: the spirits are 'not formed in the cruor, but in the serum of the blood'. A check with the cross-referenced entries, such as BLOOD, BODY, BRAIN, CIRCULATION, FIBRE, FLUID, MUSCULAR, NERVE, PART, SECRETION, SENSORIUM, SENSORY,

SOUL, shows Chambers oscillating between scepticism and the confession that the spirits seem useful, if only to save appearances; without them there seems to be a gap in nature. His doubts are revealed by the inconsistency and contradiction of his definitions. Under ANIMAL we read that

> ANIMAL *spirits* are a fine subtile juice, or humour in animal bodies; supposed to be the great instrument of muscular motion, sensation, &c. . . .
>
> The ancients distinguished spirits into three kinds, *viz.*, *animal, vital* and *vegetative*; but the moderns have reduced them to one sort, *viz., animal*, about the nature of which, and the matter whence they are formed, great disputes have arisen among anatomists, though their existence has never been fairly proved. . . .
>
> However, the antiquity of the opinion claims some reverence.

The conflicting claims of ancient opinion and the new science could hardly be summarized more neatly. The disparity between the different entries, SPIRITS and ANIMAL SPIRITS, is enough to illustrate a theory uncertainly poised between the medical and the metaphysical. By the time Sterne made use of it, more than twenty years later, it was moribund.

David Hartley's *Observations on Man* (1749) says:

> And thus we seem to approach to all that is probable in the received doctrines concerning the nervous Fluid, and the animal Spirits, supposed to be either the same or different Things, and all the Arguments which *Boerhaave* has brought for his Hypothesis, of a glandular secretion of a very subtle active Fluid in the Brain, may be accommodated to the *Newtonian* Hypothesis of Vibrations.[11]

Hartley applied to human physiology Newton's theory that 'a very subtle and elastic Fluid, which he calls Æther, . . . is diffused through the Pores of gross Bodies, as well as through the open Spaces that are void of gross Matter.'[12]

According to Chambers, the word 'spirit' in 'Newtonian physics . . . denotes a most subtile penetration of substance'. Substance here is not merely inert matter, but one of the Aristotelian categories. And as A. D. Nuttall points out:

> In the middle ages the word was frequently used to denote spirit, especially God himself as the supreme substance. After

the sixteenth century it came to be reserved, almost exclusively for material substance.[13]

To a confusing degree, the new science borrowed the vocabulary of the scholasticism it repudiated.

The scientist Robert Boyle (1627–91), experimenting on respiration, rejected the belief that air, taken in by the lungs, was transmuted into 'vital spirits'.

The Anatomy of Melancholy, a favourite with Sterne, has a good deal to say about the animal spirits, which Burton links with 'the common division of the soul . . . into three principal faculties, vegetal, sensitive and rational'.[14] The brain contains 'the receptacles of the spirits, brought hither by the arteries from the heart, and are there more refined to a more heavenly nature, to perform the actions of the soul.'[15] Spirit is 'a common tie or medium betwixt the body and the soul; or, as Paracelsus, a fourth soul of itself'.[16]

For John Donne, the spirits were 'that subtile knot, which makes us man' ('The Exstasie'). The animal spirits, if not quite to be identified with the soul, were understood to be mysteriously and mystically linked with it. But after the publication of Descartes's *Treatise on the Passions* in 1649, the animal spirits were increasingly thought of as physical entities. For Descartes, they were merely little animals in the bloodstream, and he boldly located the soul in the pineal gland. That Sterne was aware of Descartes's opinion we know from Volume 2, Chapter 19, p. 173/p. 117, and also from the Abbess of Quedlingberg's erotic dream in Slawkenbergius's Tale:

> the courteous stranger's nose had got perched upon the top of the pineal gland of her brain, and made such rousing work. . . . (Vol. 4, p. 301/p.203)[17]

Locke's two references to the animal spirits in his *Essay Concerning Human Understanding* make it clear he considers them as material:

> Impressions made on a heap of atoms, or animal spirits, are altogether as useful and render the subject as noble, as the thoughts of a soul. . . .'[18]

> . . . 'tis evident that some motion must thence be continued by our Nerves or animal Spirits, there to *produce in our Minds the Particular* Ideas. . . .[19]

That the animal spirits were pretty well materialized and secularized by 1749, we know from Fielding's jocular reference in *Tom Jones*, where they seem to be equated with libido:

> Jones had naturally violent animal spirits; these being set on float and augmented by the spirit of wine, produced most extravagant effects. He kissed the doctor and embraced him with the most passionate endearments. . . .[20]

By 1880, the term had lost all living reference. Canon Daniel, editor of Locke's *Thoughts Concerning Education*, can do no better than gloss 'animal spirits' as 'nervous energy', the meaning the term retains today, insofar as it is used at all now that medical theory has no further use for it.

3

Sterne's link with contemporary medical thought, however, was problematical in this instance. Tristram's miserably diminished animal spirits, his fragility, are part of a wider imaginative and referential web, for which Sterne was drawing, as usual, on older traditions of learning. For Rabelais, the animal spirits endow us with 'imagination, discourse, judgement, resolution, deliberation, ratiocination and memory'.[21] (The original French has verbs where the translators have supplied nouns: *'les esprits animaulx, moyennans les quels elle imagine, discourt, juge, resoust, delibère, ratiocine et rememore'*.) But Sterne was using the Urquhart-Motteux-Ozell translation and its list is echoed in Volume 4, Chapter 27, when Phutatorius receives the hot chestnut where it hurts him most.

> —the soul of *Phutatorius*, together with all his ideas . . . his imagination, judgment, resolution, deliberation, ratiocination, memory, fancy, with ten batallions of animal spirits, all tumultuously crouded down, through different defiles and circuits, to the place in danger, leaving all his upper regions, as you may imagine, as empty as my purse. (p. 382/p. 257)

Damage to the animal spirits, then, like damage to the genitals (a misfortune which happens both to Phutatorius and to Tristram) is a serious matter. The reasons for Tristram's debility become clearer. Gardner D. Stout, Jr., observes that the effect of Mrs. Shandy's 'unseasonable question', to have

> scattered and dispersed the animal spirits, whose business it was to have escorted and gone hand-in-hand with the *HOMUNCULUS*, and conducted him safe to the place destined for his reception . . . (Vol. 1, Ch. 2, p. 2/p. 6)

is a paraphrase of Rabelais. Stout, having noted the parallel, leaves the matter there. He draws no interpretive conclusions, makes no attempt to relate Rabelais's revealing definition of the 'animal spirits' to Sterne's novel as a whole.[22] The differences in context, however, between the Rabelais passage and Sterne's use of it are crucial to full understanding of *Tristram Shandy*. Rabelais writes that

> the fervency of lust is abated by certain drugs, plants, herbs and roots, which make the Taker cold, maleficiated, unfit for and unable to perform the act of generation . . . the water-lilly, *Heraclea, Agnus-Castus*, Willow-twigs, Hemp-stalks, Woodbind, Honeysuckle, Tamarisk, Chast-tree, Mandrake, Bennet, Kecbugloss, the Skin of Hippopotamus . . . which . . . do either mortify and beclumpse with cold the prolific semence, or scatter and disperse the Spirits; which ought to have gone along with and conducted the Sperm to the Places destinated and appointed for its Reception.[23]

The reader who knows his Rabelais and picks up the echoes is alerted at once. In Rabelais it is a cooling diet of herbs which dissipates the guardian spirits, by damaging the generative functions of the male. Walter Shandy is an enthusiast for these anti-genial specifics. Writing to his brother Toby to warn him against the attractions of the Widow Wadman, Walter recommends a diet drawn from Burton but which shows a family resemblance to the coolants listed (above) by Rabelais.

> As for thy drink—I need not tell thee, it must be the infusion of VERVAIN, and the herb HANEA, of which Ælian relates such effects—but if thy stomach palls with it—discontinue it from time to time, taking cucumbers, melons, purslane, water-lillies, woodbine and lettice. (Vol. 8, Ch. 34, p. 728/p. 478)

Lettuce was a well-known soporific. When allowed to bolt, its boiled leaves produce an opium-like substance which induces heavy sleep or even coma.

The Anatomy of Melancholy recommends as cooling

> ... Cowcumbers, Melons, Purselan, Water-lilies, Rue, Wood-bine, Ammi, Lettice ... *Athenian* women, in their solemn feasts called *Thesmophoria*, were to abstain nine days from the company of men, during which time, saith Aelian, they laid a certain herb named *Hanea*, in their beds, which assuaged those ardent flames of love, and freed them from the torments of that violent passion.[24]

This passage is agreed to be the source of reference in Walter's letter since, according to A. H. Bullen, editor of Burton, Hanea can only be an error for Greek *agnea*, or *agnos*. We are back with Rabelais's *Agnus-Castus*, which Chambers defines as

> a medicinal shrub, having a monopetalous flower, and narrow digital leaf; famous among the ancients as a specific for the preservation of chastity, and the preventing of all venereal desires, pollutions &c., ... the Athenian ladies, who made professions of chastity, lay upon leaves of Agnus Castus, during the feast of Ceres.
>
> It is reputed a cooler, and particularly of the genital parts; and was anciently used in physic to allay those inordinate motions arising from seminal tumescence, but it is out of the present practice.

Walter characteristically recommends obsolete medicines. In the case of Vervain, he seems to have slipped up: the joke is on Walter, as Vervain was a magical, merry-making herb, used for love-potions.[25]

The Grete Herball printed by Peter Treveris 1526–29 (translated from the French, *Le Grant Herbier*) has:

> To make folke mery at ye table, take foure leves foure rotes vervayn wyne than spryncle the wyne all about the hous where the eatinge is they shall be all mery.[26]

Hieronymus Bock, writing in 1498, said that Verbena (another name for Vervain) was 'for magic rather than medicine'.[27]

Coolants are similarly under discussion in an elusive and more than usually ambiguous chapter: Volume 6, Chapter 36. Tristram seems to be the speaker, but he echoes his father's thought and phrasing (as he often does) in his incoherent mammerings as to whether or not love is a disease. Treatment, he says, consists of

> a cooling glyster of hempseed and bruised cucumbers;—and
> followed on with thin potations of water lillies and purslane—
> to which he added a pinch of snuff, of the herb *Hanea*;— . . .
> (p. 563/374)

a familiar list of sexual depressants, guaranteed, according to Rabelais, to dissipate the spirits. Tristram says his father's mind will be busy with such matters, since Walter 'had laid in a great stock of knowledge of this kind'. Walter's theories of love, adds Tristram, 'contrived to crucify my Uncle *Toby*'s mind, almost as much as his amours themselves'. Well they might. Walter's fear of sensuality is excessive. Cooling herbs, which damp down desire, freeze up the active powers of sperm, and scatter the animal spirits (that is, everything energetic, creative and fertile), seem to be the last thing needed in the Shandy family.

Walter's letter to Toby is written on the way to bed. He observes 'I had been well content that thou should'st have dipp'd the pen this moment into the ink, instead of myself . . .' (Vol. 8, Ch. 34, p. 725/p. 476). The innuendo is that Walter wishes he could delegate the job of lovemaking. Some critics have seen Walter as frustrated by his wife's sexual apathy. My own reading is that the problem is less her 'frigidity' than Walter's diminishing potency. He fails, disastrously, to engage her attention during intercourse; she finds his attentions, which occur only once a month, so boring she starts chattering *in medias res*. This would seem to be his fault. Walter distrusts the life of the body and over-values intellect. He is pathologically anxious to damp down sexuality in himself and in those close to him, tricking the tailor into spoiling Toby's breeches (Vol. 6, Ch. 36, p. 564/p. 374). As Professor Work explains, the effect of camphor (introduced on waxed cloth instead of the buckram normally used for stiffening and reinforcement in tailoring) was that '*membrum flaccidum reddit*'. The cooling herbs Walter recommends to Toby are, as we have seen, anti-life. So is Walter's mad rationality. Crazed with words, victim of the association of ideas, a severed head, Walter reacts to family crisis with historical disquisitions, rambling, incoherent, held together only by random links of memory and leading nowhere. Trim reacts to Bobby's death with the language of true feeling: such honest simplicity is beyond Walter. Like Molière's fanatics, Walter lacks *le bon sens du peuple*. Like them, he is comically exposed by the comparison. We are told early what to think: '. . . like all systematick reasoners, he would move both heaven and earth, and twist and torture every thing in nature to support his hypothesis' (Vol. 1, Ch. 19, p. 61/p. 45).

Since Walter's own animal spirits are running low at the time of Tristram's conception, the dispersal of the meagre inheritance which should have been his son's *en route* to the womb is doubly unfortunate. There was nothing

> . . . left to found thy stamina in, but negations . . . when the few animal spirits I was worth in the world, and with which memory, fancy, and quick parts should have been convey'd,— were all dispersed, confused, confounded, scattered and sent to the devil.—(Vol. 4, Ch. 19 p. 354/p. 236)

This lament, too, echoes Locke, who, in the passage cited above, wrote that the spirits were 'scattered and confounded' by a sudden fright.

Walter finds it irritating that Mrs. Shandy does not, in the general way, ask questions. But she does ask one that precipitates the chain of events which controls the wayward plot of the novel, in recounting which Sterne blends his arcane lore in characteristically idiosyncratic, antiquarian wit. As Dr. John Ferriar observed in 1798, Sterne laughed at 'exploded opinions and forsaken fooleries'.[28] But on which side of our faces do we laugh with him, when we consider Tristram's plight and our own?

NOTES

1. Nathaniel Highmore, *The History of Generation* (London: John Martin, 1651), p. 27.
2. Ibid., p. 111.
3. John Locke, *Locke's Thoughts Concerning Education*, ed. E. Daniel (London, 1880), Sect. 14. § 115 ('On Fear and Courage in Children'), pp. 221–22.

Tristram and the Animal Spirits

4. Friedrich Hoffman, *Fundamenta medicinae* (1695), transl. Lester Snow King (London: McDonald and Elsevier, 1971), p. 37.
5. F. M. Cornford (transl. with commentary), *The Republic of Plato* (Oxford: Clarendon Press, 1941), p. 127.
6. Aristotle, *De Anima*, Bk. 2, Ch. 2, §413^{b}11.
7. St. Thomas Aquinas, *Commentary on De Anima*, version of William of Moerbeke, transl. Kenelm Foster and Silvester Humphries (London: Routledge and Kegan Paul, 1951), Lectio 5, §280, p. 198.
8. E. M. W. Tillyard, *The Elizabethan World Picture* (London: Chatto and Windus, 1943), p. 64. For the Cartesian and Newtonian uses of the animal spirits, see Hillel Schwartz, *Knaves, Fools, Madmen and that Subtile Effluvium: A Study of the Opposition to the French Prophets in England, 1706–1710* (Gainsville: University Presses of Florida, 1978). Professor Schwartz points out that irregular motion of the spirits, it was believed, caused hysteria, the vapours, madness, hypochondria; if they rushed about violently, they caused convulsions and delirium; obstructions to their flow could lead to palsy (pp. 31–5).
9. Thomas S. Hall (ed.), *A Sourcebook of Animal Biology* (New York: McGraw Hill, 1951), p. 105.
10. Robert Fludd, *Opera* (Oppenheim, 1617–19), *Utriusque Cosmi Historia*, *passim*.
11. David Hartley, *Observations on Man* (London, 1749), Pt. 1, Sect. 1, Prop. 5, p. 20.
12. Ibid., p. 13.
13. A. D. Nuttall, *A Common Sky* (London: Sussex University Press, 1974), p. 19. I am grateful to Dr. Roy Porter for reminding me that the picture is complicated and that 'spirit' and 'aether' both survived into nineteenth-century physical science.
14. Robert Burton, *The Anatomy of Melancholy* (1621), ed. A. H. Bullen (London: G. Bell and Sons, 1893), Pt. 1, Sect. 1, Subsect. 5, p. 177.
15. Ibid., Pt. 1, Sect. 1, Subsect. 4, p. 176.
16. Ibid., Pt. 1, Sect. 1, Subsect. 2, p. 170.
17. See James Aiken Work's edition of *TS* (New York: Odyssey Press, 1940), p. 147 n. See also Mark Loveridge, *Laurence Sterne and the Argument About Design* (London: Macmillan, 1982), Ch. 5. Dr. W. G. Day assures me that Sterne's knowledge of Descartes was confined to what he could read in Chambers.
18. John Locke, *E.C.H.U.*, Bk. 2, Ch. 1, p. 112.
19. Ibid., Bk. 2, Ch. 5, p. 136.
20. Henry Fielding, *Tom Jones* (1749), Wesley University edition, ed. Battestin and Bowers (Oxford: Clarendon Press, 1974), Bk. 5, Ch. 9, p. 252.
21. François Rabelais, *Gargantua and Pantagruel*, transl. Urquhart-Motteux, with notes by Mr. Ozell (London: J. Brindley, 1737), Bk. 3, Ch. 4, p. 28.
22. Gardner D. Stout, Jr. 'Some borrowings in Sterne from Rabelais and Cervantes', *E.L.N.*, III (1965–66), 111.
23. Rabelais, Bk. 3, Ch. 31, p. 205.
24. Burton, Pt. 3, Sect. 2, Subsect. 1, p. 221. See James Aiken Work's *TS*, p. 468 n. He observes the herbs listed were standard 'refrigerants'.

25. Work says Vervain was 'formerly used as a cooling remedy' (p. 593 n), but cites no evidence. The *Oxford Book of Wild Flowers* says Vervain was 'used for love potions'. The *O.E.D.* cites Fletcher, *Faithfull Shepherd*, II.i: 'And thou light Varvin too, Thou must go after,/Provoking easie souls to mirth and laughter.'

26. Cited Agnes Arber, *Herbals, Their Origin and Evolution: A Chapter in the History of Botany* 1470–1670 (Cambridge: Cambridge University Press, 1912), p. 42.

27. Ibid., p. 57.

28. John Ferriar, *Illustrations of Sterne* (London: Cadell and Davies, 1798), p. 182. Dr. Ferriar points out, for example, that Sterne's black page derives from Robert Fludd's emblem of the chaos in *Utriusque Cosmi historia*. Mark Loveridge, in *Laurence Sterne and the Argument About Design*, discusses the links between eighteenth-century scientific thought and the medieval system of analogical correspondences.

Part Three:

INTERPRETATION

8

Tristram Shandy and the Art of Gossip

by BRUCE STOVEL

After three tantalizing chapters which allude to an un-
paralleled interruption, lament the terrible vulnerability of the
HOMUNCULUS, and describe the way in which knowledge
of this interruption has been handed down, the narrator of
Tristram Shandy promises in the fourth chapter that we will
finally be 'let into the whole secret from first to last'. First,
though, he warns readers who are not 'curious and inquisitive'
to skip over the remaining part of the chapter. Having thus
ensured our continued attention, he then makes a distinctive
gesture and, like the wife of King Midas, whispers the secret
knowledge:

—————————Shut the door.—————————

> I was begot in the night, betwixt the first *Sunday* and the first
> *Monday* in the month of *March*, in the year of our Lord one
> thousand seven hundred and eighteen. I am positive I was.—
> But how I came to be so very particular in my account of a
> thing which happened before I was born, is owing to another
> small anecdote known only in our family, but now made public
> for the better clearing up this point. (Vol. 1, Ch. 4, p. 6/p. 8)

Tristram, it seems clear, is adopting the stance and tone of a
gossip—the sort of person Samuel Johnson characterized in
his dictionary as 'one who runs about tattling like women at a

lying-in.' This essay will argue that Sterne, who began *Tristram Shandy* four years after the appearance of Johnson's *Dictionary*, recreated in his novel the satisfactions found in the familiar, everyday activity of gossiping. Sterne must have been struck by the fact that the realistic novel, as it had been developed by Defoe, Richardson, and Fielding, possessed some striking similarities in material and treatment to gossip.[1] In *Tristram Shandy* he seems to have decided to exploit the forms and conventions of gossip, partly in order to show the strange ways in which daily life and sophisticated art interpenetrate each other.

Interpretation consists of placing a text within a context; if we consider *Tristram Shandy* within the context of gossip, we can see that both text and context have the same subject, substance, purpose, structure, narrative situation, style, and tone. I would like to develop each one of these resemblances in turn; in doing so, a more precise sense of what gossip is, as well as what its usefulness as an interpretive tool might be, will emerge.

For my purposes, gossip is informal and casual talk between two or more people about the private lives of other people known to them.[2] The subject of gossip—my first resemblance—is thus the racy, the naughty, the veiled: things like Walter Shandy's misconception of his son, or Toby Shandy's disillusioning discovery about the opposite sex, or Tristram's unplanned circumcision, or how Uncle Toby acquired his modesty, or how Trim and Bridget managed between them to break the bridge to pieces. As these instances suggest, gossip deals most often with sexual incidents, with the kind of 'small anecdote' that women would discuss at a lying-in. This is because the most concealed part of our lives is that for which we reserve the term private parts. Even when its material is not sexual, gossip consists of domestic facts about other people which those people would not willingly discuss publicly. Gossip exists at second or third hand because self-analysis is too rigorous, confession too intense, for its relaxed and impulsive mood. Gossip is small talk, idle chitchat. Tristram thus tells us about his family and not himself; even when he recounts his own experience, he almost always makes it plain that he is not recounting his own experience first hand, but, as in the opening, reporting what his Uncle Toby has told him that his father said, or, later in Volume 1 (Ch. 16), what Uncle Toby has repeated of Tristram's mother's complaints. The nature of gossip dictates, then, that *The Life and Opinions of Tristram Shandy* will be almost all opinions and almost no life, since Tristram's own life is present as merely another occasion for gossip.

To turn from subject to substance: there is a related reason why the novel will consist almost entirely of opinions. If gossip claims as its subject what Tristram calls 'the whole secret', or what we might call the bare facts, the facts are only a starting-point for detached speculation, hypothetical connections, possible explanations. The novel's epigraph from Epictetus is especially true of gossip: 'It is not actions, but opinions concerning actions, which disturb men.' Gossip is by its very nature inconclusive, since it can no longer exist if all the facts to be explored are public knowledge. The subject, or topics, that characterize gossip are thus less important than its substance, or object. The object of speculation is knowledge of the true characters of other people, an object which can never be fully and finally attained (in real life, anyway), since, as Tristram points out, we have no window into the souls of others: 'our minds shine not through the body, but are wrapt up here in a dark covering of uncrystalized flesh and blood; so that if we would come to the specifick characters of them, we must go some other way to work' (Vol. 1, Ch. 23, p. 83/p. 60). Going to work that other way, gossip makes its necessary limitation its source of delight. How much the imagination can do with a few suggestive facts! With, for instance, an unaccountable obliquity in the way a boy sets up his top (Vol. 1, Ch. 3). If Tristram chooses to present a rare glimpse of his adult experience, all is conveyed by one fact: we see him 'as I stood with my garters in my hand, reflecting upon what had *not* passed' (Vol. 7, Ch. 29). This substance of gossip, the play of conjecture, is present in the novel at two levels. It exists within the anecdotes that Tristram reports to us, as when we see Yorick's parishioners busy speculating upon his riding habits, his help to the midwife, and the relationship between the two, or when we see the Strasburgers of Volume 4 speculating on just what the long nose of the stranger might mean. Such speculation is also a very important part of our relationship as fellow gossipers with Tristram; in this relationship, which might be called the novel's frame-tale, Tristram again and again teases us into speculation by putting before us intriguing facts: the precise nature of Uncle Toby's wound, for instance, or just what Toby was looking at when he declared that he did not know the right end of a woman (Vol. 2, Ch. 7), or exactly where and how Toby laid down his pipe when Trim told him the naked truth about the Widow Wadman (Vol. 9, Ch. 31).

We can now consider the purpose of gossip. It has none, at least no ostensible purpose. Performed for its own sake, for sheer pleasure, gossip lacks concrete purpose or explicit justification; it is a play time for the mind and has the same relation to serious discourse as play does to work. Gossip, in fact, is so enjoyable that almost all of us spend a great deal of our waking lives doing it; this pleasure is so unadulterated by usefulness that we almost all feel guilt about the time we spend gossiping ourselves, and regard the sight of other people doing so with an uneasy mixture of contempt and fear. Johnson's dictionary definition captures precisely this scorn—and yet we remember that it comes from a man who loved to gossip and did so with unforgettable flair. Of course, considered philosophically, every work of literature is play in its relation to real life. Yet some works magnify and celebrate their status as play, while others minimize it in order to concentrate upon other satisfactions; *Tom Jones* and *Clarissa* serve as opposites in this respect, as in so many others. Sterne's novel is clearly at Fielding's end of this spectrum. Tristram puts his readers into the playful, pleasure-seeking attitude that characterizes gossip; we find ourselves in the same frame of mind as Walter Shandy, who suggests that, 'as we have nothing better to do, at least till Obadiah gets back', we might as well extract some pleasure from what is at hand—in this case, a sermon on conscience (Vol. 2, Ch. 15). Again and again, in fact, Tristram presents within the novel something that was originally a serious communication, but is now transformed into a vehicle for gossip; the sermon, which Sterne himself had preached, is the outstanding example. Other instances include the judgement of the Sorbonne theologians about infant baptism

(Vol. 1, Ch. 20), the curse of Ernulphus (Vol. 3, Ch. 11), and even, amusingly, a witty passage from Rabelais describing intellectual gymnasts which is inserted *verbatim* and thus made one degree more playful (Vol. 5, Ch. 29). As Sterne says in the epigraph to Volumes 3 and 4, 'it has always been my purpose to pass from the gay to the serious and from the serious to the gay.' The effect of this shiftiness is to intensify the novel's gaiety and undermine its seriousness; as Elizabeth Drew remarks, 'Sterne was unique in his own day and unlike any major novelist since in making no pretensions to be doing anything but enjoy himself and entertain his readers.'[3] On the very first page of the novel we see—or, more precisely, hear—Tristram converting serious facts into the playful, pleasurable stuff of gossip:

> —you have all, I dare say, heard of the animal spirits, as how they are transfused from father to son, &c. &c.—and a great deal to that purpose:—Well, you may take my word, that nine parts in ten of a man's sense or his nonsense, his successes and miscarriages in this world depend upon their motions and activity, and the different tracks and trains you put them into; so that when they are once set a-going, whether right or wrong, 'tis not a halfpenny matter,—away they go cluttering like hey-go-mad; and by treading the same steps over and over again, they presently make a road of it, as plain and as smooth as a garden-walk, which, when they are once used to, the Devil himself sometimes shall not be able to drive them off it. (Vol. 1, Ch. 1, pp. 1–2/p. 5)

In structure, a bout of gossip is unsystematic, casual, and impulsive: ostensibly formless. Organized exposition belongs to the work world, not that of play; the demand for pleasure requires that gossip must move in rapid and unpredictable leaps, circling constantly about certain fascinating and never fully understood facts. Gossip concentrates upon character and disregards formal plot. All of this, of course, is strikingly applicable to *Tristram Shandy*. Tristram, for instance, explains at the end of Volume 1:

> What these perplexities of my uncle *Toby* were,—'tis impossible for you to guess;—if you could,—I should blush; not as a relation,—not as a man,—nor even as a woman,—but I

should blush as an author; inasmuch as I set no small store by myself upon this very account, that my reader has never yet been able to guess at any thing. And in this, Sir, I am of so nice and singular a humour, that if I thought you was able to form the least judgment or probable conjecture to yourself, of what was to come in the next page,—I would tear it out of my book. (Vol. 1, Ch. 25, p. 89/p. 63)

The novel, thus, has an even more wayward structure than the narrator's squiggly lines at the end of volume VI would suggest. Two further implications of gossip's formless form can be related to *Tristram Shandy*. Any given interchange of gossipers is never completed in the way that works of art are: rather, the exchange swells and shrinks to fit the time available, and, in most cases, just as Tristram does with his uncle Toby's amours, the choicest morsel is saved for the last contribution. *Tristram Shandy* is thus finished, not completed, by its final volume. A second implication is that interruption is, paradoxically, the one clear principle of connection in gossip, since gossip rejects logical coherence in favour of idle, whimsical mental association. The book opens and closes with an interruption, and Tristram advances his story through every imaginable kind of interruption; he is so ingenious in doing so that, at one point in the novel, one of his own characters interrupts *him* when he is expatiating upon the nature of love:

It is a great pity—but 'tis certain from every day's observation of man, that he may be set on fire like a candle, at either end—provided there is a sufficient wick standing out; if there is not—there's an end of the affair; and if there is—by lighting it at the bottom, as the flame in that case has the misfortune generally to put out itself—there's an end of the affair again.

For my part, could I always have the ordering of it which way I would be burnt myself—for I cannot bear the thoughts of being burnt like a beast—I would oblige a housewife constantly to light me at the top; for then I should burn down decently to the socket; that is, from my head to my heart, from my heart to my liver, from my liver to my bowels, and so on by the meseraick veins and arteries, through all the turns and lateral insertions of the intestines and their tunicles, to the blind gut—

—I beseech you, doctor Slop, quoth my uncle Toby, interrupting him as he mentioned the *blind gut*, in a discourse with my father the night my mother was brought to bed of me—I beseech you, quoth my uncle Toby, to tell me which is the blind gut; for, old as I am, I vow I do not know to this day where it lies. (Vol. 8, Ch. 15, p. 674/p. 446).

Tristram's novel begins with (in a punning sense, at least) *coitus interruptus* and proceeds by *discursus interruptus.*[4]

If gossip consists mostly of narrative, both factual and conjectural, then the situation in which this fitful narrative is created is worth examining. Gossip is indulged in by people who know each other and, in fact, get to know each other better through the act of gossiping, since, in doing so, they are pooling their knowledge, exposing their values and assumptions, and moving tentatively toward a common viewpoint. This coming to know each other on the part of the gossipers is, I suspect, the real purpose of gossip, the real social function that it serves. Gossip is thus only apparently aimless. Certainly Tristram himself holds forth the promise of just such mutual knowledge; he tells us at the start of the novel:

> I have undertaken, you see, to write not only my life, but my opinions also; hoping and expecting that your knowledge of my character, and of what kind of mortal I am, by the one, would give you a better relish for the other: As you proceed further with me, the slight acquaintance which is now beginning betwixt us, will grow into familiarity; and that, unless one of us is in fault, will terminate in friendship.—*O diem praeclarum!*— then nothing which has touched me will be thought trifling in its nature, or tedious in its telling. (Vol. 1, Ch. 6, p. 9/p. 10)

Gossip not only requires a spoken voice, that is, physical exchange, but it creates a special kind of intimacy: it not only conjectures about what takes place behind closed doors, but itself takes place when the door is shut against those outside. Tristram himself, of course, enters into just such an intimate friendship with us.[5] Furthermore, we cannot help contrasting our playful relationship with Tristram, in which there is just such a slow and steady growth into mutual understanding, with the relationships within the novel, all of which are marked by an attempt at serious exchange and by almost total frustration in that attempt; the fluid ease with which we and Tristram develop a common understanding in the frame-tale

121

is highlighted by the misunderstandings which exist within that frame.

Gossip also has its own distinctive style. As we have seen, that style is spoken; even when gossip occurs in letters and not in person, the letters reproduce the patterns of spontaneous speech, not those of formal prose. Furthermore, gossip employs a distinctive kind of spoken style: allusive, full of veiled reference and innuendo, of nuance and *double entendre*. It is somehow very pleasant to convey the most charged facts without ever having been indiscreet enough to name them outright. Tristram, for instance, in the chapter of explanation with which I began, employs just this knowing sort of suggestiveness when he describes the cause of his mother's inopportune question:

> My father . . . had made it a rule for many years of his life,—on the first *Sunday night* of every month throughout the whole year,—as certain as ever the *Sunday night* came,—to wind up a large house-clock which we had standing upon the back-stairs head, with his own hands:—And being somewhere between fifty and sixty years of age, at the time I have been speaking of,—he had likewise gradually brought some other little family concernments to the same period, in order, as he would often say to my uncle *Toby*, to get them all out of the way at one time, and be no more plagued and pester'd with them the rest of the month. . . .
>
> My poor mother could never hear the said clock wound up,—but the thoughts of some other things unavoidably popp'd into her head,—& *vice versâ*: . . . (Vol. 1, Ch. 4, pp. 6–7/ pp. 8–9)

This allusive shorthand allows for a shared play between those gossiping; the reader's imagination must be ready to give ordinary words a richer texture and fuller meaning. Tristram describes the style of his novel, and its origin in the nature of gossip, in just these terms:

> Writing, when properly managed, (as you may be sure I think mine is) is but a different name for conversation: As no one, who knows what he is about in good company, would venture to talk all;—so no author, who understands the just boundaries of decorum and good breeding, would presume to think all: The truest respect which you can pay to the reader's

understanding, is to halve this matter amicably, and leave him
something to imagine, in his turn, as well as yourself. (Vol. 2,
Ch. 11, p. 125/p. 87)

My final point is that gossip has a distinctive tone or mood,
one that, as I have suggested, is intimate, secretive, relaxed,
detached, playful, impulsive, zestful. Each one of these
adjectives describes both the characteristic mood of gossip and
the special atmosphere, indeed the special appeal, of *Tristram
Shandy*. This mood creates, or at least intensifies, friendships
by its atmosphere of shared delight; Tristram holds before us
the prospect that, as friends, we will eventually not only
understand each other, but have a better relish for each other.
This mood of shared delight in speculative contemplation
magnifies the importance of the gossipers at the expense of
those who are being gossiped about. For the talkers to grow,
those discussed must become smaller (whence, by the way, the
vague fear that we feel when we see friends talking idly on a
street corner). We can note that, beginning with the
HOMUNCULUS, every character in *Tristram Shandy* is
belittled: Walter Shandy, his wife, Uncle Toby, the Widow
Wadman, even Yorick, even Tristram. It is hard to imagine
how any character could be presented within the novel and
not be comically diminished by becoming a source of gossipy
anecdote and speculation.[6]
    To recapitulate, I believe that *Tristram Shandy* transforms
into art the real-life experience of gossip, and that the novel's
distinctive subject, substance, purpose, structure, narrative
situation, style, and mood recreate that experience. When we
recall the puritanical reaction that almost all of us have at the
sight of other people tattling together like women at a lying-in,
we can see why F. R. Leavis dismissed Sterne in a footnote to
the opening pages of *The Great Tradition* as a nasty and
irresponsible trifler.
    If this perception of the importance of gossip to *Tristram
Shandy* is valid, it helps explain a number of puzzling facts
about this most puzzling of novels; I would like to examine one
of these puzzles by way of a conclusion, or perhaps I should
say, finish. Not many readers in recent years have found
Tristram Shandy lacking in moral seriousness, as Leavis does,

but an increasing number have found the novel very serious in another way, as a presentation of a philosophy of art. In the most persuasive and searching of these accounts, Robert Alter constructs a great tradition of his own, a counter-version of the novel's development.[7] Alter is interested in the novel that concentrates its imaginative energy upon depicting its own complex relationship with the real world; Sterne forms an important link in this tradition, which begins with Cervantes, and moves through to Nabokov, Barth, and Fowles in our day. But Alter, and those who approach *Tristram Shandy* as he does, omit to mention one striking fact: Sterne never suggests, as Cervantes, Nabokov, *et al.* do so pervasively, that all of the events and characters of *his* books are made up. Fielding, for instance, Sterne's great predecessor in the English comic novel, repeatedly reminds us that we are enjoying the sophisticated pleasures of imaginary events, not a straightforward transcription of real experience; the very first words of the narrative of *Tom Jones* force this awareness upon us—'In that part of the western division of this kingdom, which is commonly called Somersetshire, there lately lived (and perhaps lives still) a gentleman whose name was Allworthy. . . .'—and we all recall the slyness of Book XVII, Chapter 1 of *Tom Jones*, in which the narrator laments his hero's apparently inevitable doom, and hopes that Tom can be extricated from his calamities by natural and credible means. Tristram, however, never allows such reflections to arise, and a glance at Nabokov will assure us that Sterne's choice of first-person narration is not a sufficient explanation for this lack of Cervantesque irony. How could a man with Sterne's subtle and playful mind, a man who knew and admired *Don Quixote*, fail to recreate such an important element in Cervantes' appeal? Fielding, we note, seizes upon and elaborates just this element. The answer, I suspect, resides in the paradoxical nature of gossip; while its substance is largely hypothesis, as I have argued, those hypotheses are meant to account for real events and real causes in our own experience. This is precisely why gossip is so disreputable, while fiction, so similar in many ways, is comparatively respectable.[8] The hypotheses of gossip are provisional; what they try to explain is real. After all, why shut the door and whisper the whole secret if you, and your secret, are admittedly imaginary?

'Tristram Shandy' and the Art of Gossip

NOTES

1. Several critics have noticed this resemblance. In 'The Fact in Fiction', Mary McCarthy argues that 'Even when it is most serious, the novel's characteristic tone is one of gossip and tittletattle.' See her collection of essays *On the Contrary* (New York: Farrar, Straus and Cudahy, 1961), p. 265. Homer O. Brown speculates that the realistic novel shares the formal properties of two opposed forms of communication in everyday life, gossip and letters: the first is spontaneous, communal, evanescent; the latter deliberate, individual and permanent. Brown's essay, 'The Errant Letter and the Whispering Gallery', appears in *Genre*, X (1977), 573–99.

2. My generalizations throughout this essay are indebted to two recent essays by Patricia Meyer Spacks: 'In Praise of Gossip', *Hudson Review*, XXV (1982), 19–39; 'Gossip: How it works', *Yale Review*, LXXII (1983), 561–80.

3. *The Novel: A Modern Guide to Fifteen English Masterpieces* (New York: Dell, 1963), p. 75. This view of the novel is developed in Richard A. Lanham's *Tristram Shandy: The Games of Pleasure* (Berkeley and Los Angeles: University of California Press, 1973).

4. For a provocative exploration of this notion, see J. Paul Hunter, '*Tristram Shandy* and the Art of Interruption', *Novel*, IV (1971), 132–46. The essay is reprinted in the Norton Critical Edition of *Tristram Shandy*, ed. Howard Anderson (New York: W. W. Norton, 1980), pp. 623–40.

5. 'A feature of Sterne's peculiar genius is the relationship he establishes with his readers. This is far closer to friendship, in the normal sense of that term, than any other novelist ever comes.' A. E. Dyson, *The Crazy Fabric: Essays in Irony* (London: Macmillan, 1965), p. 36. Dyson's essay first appeared as 'Sterne: The Novelist as Jester' in *Critical Quarterly*, IV (1962), 309–20.

6. Gossip has always been thought of as detraction, originating in malice. Chaucer's *Parson's Tale* considers that back-biting originates in envy and identifies five forms it commonly takes in everyday conversation (lines 490–98). Modern social science, in very different language, takes the same position: 'Gossip is a surreptitious aggression', according to Samuel Heilman, a contemporary sociologist (quoted by Spacks, 'Gossip: How It Works', p. 562).

7. *Partial Magic: The Novel as a Self-Conscious Genre* (Berkeley and Los Angeles: University of California Press, 1975).

8. Spacks makes this point: 'If the story has nothing to do with anyone we know, better, if it has nothing to do with anyone real—under such circumstances, we can enjoy it with no culpability.' 'In Praise of Gossip', p. 38.

9

Liberty in *Tristram Shandy*

by MARK LOVERIDGE

Tristram Shandy is, among other things, a dramatization of one of the classic topics of philosophical and religious debate: the question of whether or not man is free, whether he enjoys free-will in any sense that might allow him to choose to be redeemed through the operation of grace. The particular form of this debate that Sterne inherits from other eighteenth-century writers is one which explores the question of whether man's mental life is conditioned and determined by external forces to an extent which renders his responses mechanical and necessary. The first part of this essay is devoted to showing how Sterne develops this subject by means of a peculiar arrangement or selection of material, and to showing how one poetic analogue and one poetic source of *Tristram Shandy* use a similar arrangement. The second part examines a question about the structure of the book which arises as a result of this treatment of 'liberty'.

Sterne's central interests in *Tristram Shandy* lie in the forces that influence the mind, and in the comic and incongruous aspects of the drama of the mind's responses. The characters of the book appear eccentric, yet Sterne's interest in 'man' is abstract and universal. It leads him to a position where he is able to consider the readers of his work and the characters within it in the same way, as typical examples of the ways in which humanity reacts, and to develop his theme with reference to both at once. The reader gradually learns that an important part of his own rôle is to become aware of the ways in which his literary and emotional responses are being manipulated and controlled by the constant provocation of Tristram's teasing rhetoric. 'We see that we are supposed to take part with the author in the consideration of the ways in which we are influenced.'[1]

The characters, however, are much more closely under the control of the world of influences. Walter is continually at the mercy of his hypotheses, his mind's habit of producing systems of ideas. From this, and from his sense of the disasters that befall himself and his son, emerges his (and the reader's) vague consciousness of a malignant external conspiracy controlling the lives of the Shandys, the force that Tristram names as 'the ungracious Duchess . . . Fortune' (Vol. 1, Ch. 5, p. 8/ p. 10). Toby's life is ruled even more directly by his specific hobby-horse, and by his associative military reflex. Even Tristram himself will sometimes suggest, half-seriously, that he is governed by forces outside his control, especially in his writing. In some moods he will apologize for his digressions rather than praising the method: 'why do I mention it?—Ask my pen,—it governs me,—I govern not it' (Vol. 6, Ch. 6, p. 500/p. 334). He will even suggest that his apparently casual, free, digressive narrative is in fact forced on him by his public rôle of historian of the Shandys, his being a slave to the variety of his documentary sources, rather than being simply the product of his own mind. All these 'rolls, records, documents, and endless genealogies', he says; 'what a dance he may be led, by one excursion or another' (Vol. 1, Ch. 14, p. 41/p. 32).

One of the ways in which Sterne reinforces this sense of the characters suffering through the agency of external forces is by establishing a pattern in which the crises of the plot turn on the behaviour of what should be merely inanimate objects, but which become strangely active and influential. The responsible force is gravity; objects fall unexpectedly and distressingly upon the characters' bodies and minds, stimulating the characteristic patterns of reaction and motivation which form the central drama of the book. A piece of masonry falling from the besieged wall of Namur strikes Toby on or about the groin; from this (and from his character) derives his hobby-horsical study of projectiles and ballistics and his miniature battlefield.

From his hobby-horse comes a desire for metal for model demi-culverins; from this derives the crucial lack of sash weights in the window, which falls with such force upon Tristram's tenderest spot. From this accident a whole grove of reactions grows: Tristram's diabolical scream, Walter's bitter Philippick 'upon the forgetfulness of chamber-maids' (Vol. 5, Ch. 26, p. 458/p. 307), the discussions on health. The stray hot chestnut falls from the table into the aperture of Phutatorius's flies, stimulating a variety of reactive inference and motive-mongering in the assembled company. Round these central falls and blows are grouped others, literal and metaphorical: falls on to the drawbridge, on to the bed, from horses, sermons falling from volumes, Trim's histrionic dropping of his hat to call forth a response as varied as that which the chestnut produces; blows from the muleteer against the ass's bottom—the reaction to which may well be characteristic (Vol. 7, Ch. 21, p. 609/p. 406)—'blows . . . in the dark' (Vol. 1, Ch. 12, p. 34/p. 27), blows of affliction ('WHEN the misfortune of my NOSE fell so heavily upon my father's head' (Vol. 4, Ch. 17, p. 349/p. 233)), of the Duchess Fortune, from violently-ridden hobby-horses—with other related details such as the odd, coy reference to 'the line of GRAVITATION' (Vol. 6, Ch. 40, p. 572/p. 381) left dangling at the end of Volume 6.

Readers in 1760, after the publication of Volumes 1 and 2, were quite well able to see where the central theme of the book would lie, and even to anticipate the interest in gravity that this would involve. This is because gravity or 'attraction' is one of the conventional eighteenth-century analogues of the association of ideas. Sterne designed the first anecdote of the book, Mrs. Shandy's association between the winding of the clock and sexual intercourse, to raise this theme in an active, polemical way, by raising the expectation that the book's satire would involve showing man's reactions as mechanical and passive, like the clock. When the Methodist George Whitefield takes umbrage at the first two volumes, it is not 'the picture of a couple in actual *flagranti!*'[2] (to quote a different pamphlet) that disturbs him, but the association between birth and mechanism:

> Pray thou for the new birth; there will be no occasion for winding up a clock, regeneration does not depend upon wheels

and springs; it depends only on the spirit, it depends upon grace, and not upon mechanism.[3]

The author of the ingenious but bizarre 1760 pamphlet called *The Clockmakers' Outcry against* . . . *Tristram Shandy* similarly accuses Tristram of espousing 'the accursed doctrine of Materialism'[4] in Tristram's assertion in the first paragraph that his character would be determined by the timing of conception; while the author of a third pamphlet responds to the mention of 'judicial astrology, or predestination,—faith I can't tell which;—but 'tis no great matter, for they are almost the same thing'.[5] At the end of the pamphlet he has followed this theme through to discussing 'attraction', first claiming to think that it is simply an occult quality—'Behold yon madman . . . is his phrenzy greater than that of the student who thinks that the word *attraction* is a key,—and that with it he can unlock all the secrets of nature?'[6] But at the conclusion he has to retract this opinion as the critics express their horror at this unfashionable view. He ends by hoping to be *F.R.S.*:

> I believe Sir Isaac Newton to have been infallible in philosophy;—that attraction is the grand *arcanum* of nature,— and that it perfectly explains all the motions of the heavenly bodies, and all the phenomena of nature.[7]

Including, of course, the motivations and reactions of the human mind: a spectre which Sterne, along with much associationist philosophy of the eighteenth century, holds over his readers' heads, though in a rather more peculiar and sardonic fashion.

These readers are probably aware that this is not the first time this debate has been dramatized in eighteenth-century literature. Perhaps the clearest analogue of this aspect of *Tristram Shandy* is a poem, *Verses Occasioned by a Dispute in Company*, published in 1739 by a cleric and theologian, Richard Barton, at the end of a collection of satirical prose pieces called *Farrago*. The poem is cast in the form of a dramatic report of a learned symposium or debate, somewhat in the manner of the Rabelaisian symposia of *Tristram Shandy*. It develops its subject, 'Liberty in Man', through taking the association of ideas as its theme, and also using the processes of association to dramatize its points, as Sterne does.

'Twixt subtle Sophs an argument began,
Th' important theme was Liberty in Man:
And here they first remark'd, of diff'rent kind,
A passive body, and an active mind.
The body, as the mind directs, obeys;
That is not free, which can't act diff'rent ways;
A stone will ever pierce the yielding air,
Seeking th' attractive centre of its sphere;
But can't, without another impulse, move
Backward, and freely pierce the air above.
How far does this attractive pow'r extend?
Where does the force of sev'ral systems end?
Just where they end, repelling pow'rs begun,
Make all the systems one another shun,
Tho' each attracted to a central Sun,
So hard it is to make a middle state,
'Twixt love attractive, and repulsive hate.
Men are not free, who, like these systems, move,
By every passion urg'd, or hate, or love.
Passion's like wind, which fills the swelling sail;
The ship must fly before th' impelling gale.
In vain the mariner the rocks descries;
She strikes; he makes a piteous pray'r, and dies.
Pernicious wealth! for thee we plough the sea,
Delve the deep mine, and shun the face of day.
When homespun flax might clothe the beauteous bride,
Better than far-fetch'd silks, and *India*'s pride;
Sure 'tis not sense, but custom, rules mankind:
Why are not *Turks*, like us, to one confin'd?
But, hold! recal the question in debate;
This is not arguing, but rambling prate.
From ships, attraction, silk, what mortal can
Prove or disprove the Liberty of Man?
Each Soph, confounded at the just rebuke,
Gave proof of inward shame by outward look.
'When Autumn thus invites the wanton hound
To beat the furz, and try the tainted ground;
By summer's ease made keen for rural sport.
The squires and dogs to neighb'ring heaths resort:
Th' affrighted hare her secret form forsakes,
And winding ways thro' puzzling covers takes.
The dogs, transported with the new delight,
Throw up their noses, and pursue by sight:

Fallacious sight! for soon the thicket shields
The flying prey, which yet another yields;
That other's soon succeeded by fresh game;
Still they pursue another, and the same;
In vain the huntsman hallows, and the hills
Echo the rig'rous lash, whilst madness fills
Th' unruly pack——until declining Sun,
And stiffen'd sinews, must forbid to run.'[8]

Barton begins with the desired conclusion, 'A passive body and an active mind': prove this, and you prove that man's mind is 'free'. But then the poem becomes odd and difficult to match the Sophs' method of argument. As a prelude to showing that the mind is active they set out to show that the body is passive. Unfortunately the example of a passive body that they light on, the falling stone, is also emblematic of a passive mind, through the conventional analogy between gravity and the association of ideas. As they think about the stone, the Sophs begin to hurtle helplessly down a train of association of their own. Their minds seize on the analogy, grow enthusiastic, move steadily outwards to the great gravity-controlled system of the physical universe, and conclude (despite their premise) that 'Men are not free'.

Then they produce another conventional metaphor for the mind at the mercy of association, the wind-blown ship. They think that they are still talking about bodies or 'passions', emotions, rather than about mental movement, but their having recourse to all these conventional figures indicates that it is their minds that are pre-conditioned and not free. The point is made again as the Sophs produce what they take to be a mere point of argument about the ways in which 'custom' rules mankind: custom meaning the fashion for Indian silks. The 'beauteous Bride' then conjures up the Mohammedan custom of polygamy, so they use this as another example. However, the other meaning of 'custom', habit or convention, eventually occurs to them, and they can reveal to themselves that all they are doing is going down a well-marked and well-established train of ideas. 'Th' important theme' breaks up as the Sophs acquire a certain sheepish humility, obliquely aware of the limits to their 'liberty' through an awareness of their mental characteristics and limitations.

The poem then moves tangentially into an illustrative parable or analogy-by-digression. The previous action is repeated in yet another stock metaphor for mental movement, the image of dogs scenting game, or 'ranging' in the field. The dogs are the Sophs; just as the Sophs perceived analogy between apparently related objects and ideas, so the dogs perceive analogy between the successive hares they see, which they register as a single animal. Had they used their noses—their judgements—they would have smelt (claims Barton) the differences between them. As it is, the dogs are experiencing a physical equivalent of 'wit', as defined by Locke and others as the perception of casual or superficial resemblances between ideas.

It is a remarkable poem, very highly Shandean, not just in the concatenation of mind and gravity, but in the way the poem develops its subject into other Shandean areas: the dramatization of the differences between wit and judgement; the Sophs' enthusiasm and passion for the idea and for their own associations; the check they receive while in full flight ('dismounting', as Tristram would say); and doing all this by pursuing the narrative processes that *Tristram Shandy* will use, analogy, digression, illustrative parable, dramatic reporting. It is also remarkable in that there is no trace in it of the usual kind of mid-eighteenth century poem on liberty, as written by Akenside, Thomson, Collins and Warton: a form in which the social and political liberties enjoyed by Britons were praised by being set against the supposed political slavery of continental nations. Nor is it satire, because the poet uses a part of the satiric target (analogy) to make his own points and to create a new perspective.

The exemplar for this aspect of Sterne and Barton is the least satirical, most facetious of the great Augustan poets, Matthew Prior. Sterne's relations with the Augustans are usually discussed by way of the apparent similarities between *Tristram Shandy* and the Scriblerian satire of Pope and Swift. However Prior came as readily to Sterne's mind as did the other Augustans,[9] and there are very many similarities, both general and incidental, between Prior's poems and Sterne's book. Among these is the same matrix of subject, technique and motif as is found in Barton and Sterne, which occurs in Prior's long poem *Alma*.

Alma is set, again, in the form of a pert learned symposium, in this case a dialogue between two rather seedy gentlemen, Matt and Dick. They discuss the relation between body and soul, or mind, in a colloquial learned doggerel. The idea of predisposition arises from a discussion of a force called Adhesion which is supposed to operate in the body. From this develops the image of 'weight', and from this Matt derives the sad impossibility of their doing anything in the evening except going to a hostelry to drink and play cards, and then going on to visit a young lady, as usual:

> Now, RICHARD, this coercive Force,
> Without your Choice, must take its Course. . . .
> And thou and I, by Pow'r unseen,
> Are barely passive, and suck'd in
> To HENAULT's Vaults, or CELIA's Chamber. . . .
> Poor Men! poor Papers! We and They
> Do some impulsive Force obey;
> And are but play'd with:—Do not play.[10]

There can be, thinks Matt, only one cause for this:

> Thus to save further Contradiction,
> Against what You may think but Fiction;
> I for ATTRACTION, Dick, declare;
> Deny it those bold Men that dare.
> As well your Motion, as your Thought,
> Is all by hidden Impulse wrought[11]

Later, Dick uses comparisons between the mind and mechanical devices to suggest that the mind may be no more than a series of reflexes. Matt is upset, and raises the question as the first anecdote of *Tristram Shandy* does:

> Dick, from these Instances and Fetches,
> Thou maks't of Horses, Clocks and Watches,
> Quoth MAT, to me thou seems't to mean,
> That ALMA is a mere machine[12]

No, no, says Dick, and the mock-argument goes on. Towards the end the poem modulates into a less satirical, more personal mood, as the poet begins to dramatize his own attitude to the more peculiar and hobby-horsical aspects of his own mental behaviour. The earlier disquisitions on ideas and mind are used as a background against which to create a new

133

perspective, a blend of introspection, self-awareness and humility which, although it matches the movement of Barton's *Verses*, is more affecting. It moves the poem's interests away from 'mind' to something wider, something closer to character.

If *Tristram Shandy* does share subject and motif with these two poems, one might also expect Sterne to echo this aspect of their form and to create a different mood towards the end of the book as a way of resolving the subject. At first it is hard to see how this might be done, because the basic structural patterns of the book are mostly circular, digressive, repetitive and ultimately static. The critical consensus seems to be that *Tristram Shandy* does not progress or develop in any meaningful sense; the ending is typically seen as 'self-defeating . . . Given Sterne's orientation, there can be no progression'.[13] By the end of Volume 1, 'the whole parish is on scene and defined as much as ever it will be . . . the characters do not change. The whole is always before us.'[14] These effects of repetitive patterning—the motif of the falling body stimulating characteristic reactions is one such— create the perspective from which the characters are seen as satiric objects, doomed to repeat the same actions and responses in the timeless amber of the Shandean world.

There is, though, a general movement in *Tristram Shandy*, away from satire and towards a more tolerant and sympathetic attitude to the characters, something closer to 'humorous' comedy. This change can be seen simply as Sterne learning to accommodate himself to contemporary tastes by writing fashionable, sentimental comedy and outgrowing the elements of the older Augustan satire that are so much stronger in the early volumes. But it may well be a movement which is as necessary to the full development of the subject, and as deliberately created, as it was in Prior or Barton. Tristram did after all claim as early as Volume 1 that there were to be 'two contrary motions' in his writing, 'digressive, and . . . progressive too' (Vol. 1, Ch. 22, p. 81/p. 58). The best way of illustrating such a progression or development is to look briefly at some of the central episodes of Volume 9. In each of these in turn, a central character is allowed a brief moment of illumination or education about the nature of his own relationship with the world, and so achieves a brief perspective on his own character. At the same time, Sterne brings 'liberty' to the reader's mind in two or three discussions between Toby and Trim.

Volume 9 begins with that most unlikely event, Walter's sentimental education at the hands—more precisely, the fingers and eyes—of his wife. Walter and Elizabeth are found at Toby's house, delivering Walter's letter of dietary admonishment before Toby sets off to besiege the Widow Wadman. Mrs. Shandy expresses a desire to look through the keyhole at the imminent interview between the inamorati, 'out of *curiosity*' (Vol. 8, Ch. 35, p. 729/p. 479); Walter questions her motive: 'Call it, my dear, by its right name, quoth my father, and look through the key-hole as long as you will' (Vol. 9, Ch. 1, p. 735/ p. 485). At this point he is smitten by conscience, for a part of him knows that his wife is not the kind of woman to have that sort of questionable motive:

> My mother was then conjugally swinging with her left arm twisted under his right, in such wise, that the inside of her hand rested upon the back of his—she raised her fingers, and let them fall—it could scarce be call'd a tap; or if it was a tap—'twould have puzzled a casuist to say, whether 'twas a tap of remonstrance, or a tap of confession: my father, who was all sensibilities from head to foot, class'd it right—Conscience redoubled her blow—. (Vol. 9, Ch. 1, pp. 735–36/p. 485)

Again the falling body, again the *blow*; but this time on the tiniest of scales, and not as a stimulus to affliction but to knowledge of oneself and another. Mrs. Shandy is an innocent in sex as in ideas: 'A temperate current of blood ran orderly through her veins . . . in all critical moments both of the day and night alike . . . and what was not a little inconsistent, my father knew it——' (Vol. 9, Ch. 1, p. 736–37/p. 485–86). The tap of the fingers, and the subsequent tranquil gaze of her eye, reproach him, recall her nature, make him reproach himself.

The history of Walter's relationships and reactions in the rest of the novel has been much simpler than this. His 'subacid' humour has led him to respond aggressively and satirically to those around him, as he does here, but he has had no conception of the effect this has had on others, or indeed on the plot; for instance, he has no suspicion that his own character, which has made him give Dr. Slop Ernulphus's curse to read, is a proximate cause of the crushing of Tristram's nose, via the enraging of Slop. Also, his relations with his wife have been far otherwise. She has represented to him, and to the reader, merely an intellectual vacuum in the presence of which Walter's hypotheses plummet to earth like dead birds of paradise. Suddenly the rôles are momentarily reversed, and Mrs. Shandy is the active, educative partner. There are places in the earlier volumes where Toby can seem to do this (Vol. 3, Ch. 5, p. 192/p. 129 for example), but Toby's sentimental, benevolent gaze of 'inexpressible good will' at this point is merely passive, based on an inability to appreciate Walter's mood, and Walter has no choice but to respond in kind. What distinguishes this later episode is Walter's sudden, total understanding that his wife has understood and expressed something about his character; for once the blow and the falling body express the delicacy and complexity of full communication. It is no longer the Great System, merely 'the dust of a butterfly's wing' (Vol. 2, Ch. 19, p. 171/p. 116), credited at long last with a power of its own, to which Walter responds in full consciousness. Mrs. Shandy repeats her lesson in Chapter 11, in the cadence of a single word.

This is beyond sentiment, because both minds are active. There is no sentimental object, no mute sympathetic Toby. Shandean sentiment usually requires at least two passive minds, a sympathetic object and a pre-conditioned reader, predisposed to admire fine and delicate feelings. Sterne knows this, and will often hint at it in Tristram's style and attitude. A sentimental scene, whether here or in *A Sentimental Journey*, will often be developed through the use of turns of phrase which suggest partly mechanical or reflex responses. Eric Rothstein tells of Tristram being 'the helpless prey of his own "vibrations" '[15] and remarks on how often 'the celebrated pathos of his book must be put in terms of mechanics.'[16] This is not always the case: the sentimental scene may strike Tristram too unexpectedly, or involve too large a degree of conscious humour, to be tainted with hints of mechanism. But the sentimental scene in which Tristram is involved in the final volume, the meeting with Maria of Moulins, is unique in the book.

Liberty in 'Tristram Shandy'

The danger signs are all there: Maria's situation (distressed); her pipe, on which she plays; Tristram's sentimental pre-conditioning (having been thinking of Toby's amours 'I was in the most perfect state of bounty and good will; and felt the kindliest harmony vibrating within me, with every oscillation of the chaise . . . They were the sweetest notes I ever heard' (Vol. 9, Ch. 24, p. 781/p. 522)). One would expect him to be ripe for a fall of some kind, satirical or bathetic, but what actually happens takes the scene quite beyond both satire and sentiment. Tristram sits between Maria and her goat; Maria looks from one to the other:

> ——Well, Maria, said I softly——What resemblance do you find?
> I do intreat the candid reader to believe me, that it was from the humblest conviction of what a *Beast* man is . . . I would not have let fallen an unseasonable pleasantry in the venerable presence of Misery, to be entitled to all the wit that ever Rabelais scatter'd——and yet I own my heart smote me, and that I so smarted at the very idea of it, that I swore I would set up for Wisdom and utter grave sentences the rest of my days——. (Vol. 9, Ch. 24, pp. 783–84/p. 523)

Earlier in the book Tristram might have been apologetic about his method, the digressions, but never about his own character and the comic reactions it calls from him despite himself. It is a remarkable passage, dexterously evoking Tristram's self-consciousness, his awareness of his own emotional response to Maria, his sense of the incongruity of his remark and of the possibility of its being misunderstood. More than this, it expresses Tristram's awareness that this particular episode and response are characteristic of others he has made, reported or written. Through this awareness the passage manages to create the effect of Tristram seeing his own limitations in a wider, almost universal light. To this extent, Tristram is liberated from his own nature, able simultaneously to look inside himself and to consider others, and hence to learn about the representative nature of his own peculiarities. The abstractions, wit, Misery, Wisdom, man, sound quite natural and help in the fusion of critical moment with wider enlightenment. All lurking hints of mechanical response dissolve. The last effect is to evoke the distance, as well as the rapport, between Tristram and Maria; for how can he know whether he has been understood?

There are other aspects to Tristram's liberation, one of which is his freedom from those documentary sources. He always did want to write about Toby's amours, and to write dramatic episodes and illustrations rather than reproduce documents, and now he can. This is the culmination of another gradual movement in *Tristram Shandy*, away from all the forms of other people's writing, and towards Tristram being able to tell his stories in his own way. Volume 9 is almost devoid of any writing except Tristram's (Walter's letter at the end of Volume 8 is the last document) and, more remarkable, is also almost devoid of plagiarism on Sterne's part. Tristram is free to use his own words, and so is Sterne.

Tristram reserves his digression about Maria until this late point because it illustrates, by premonition, the last and most important of the moments of enlightenment, that of Toby. As with Walter and Tristram, it is an enlightenment about motives, a lesson about character. Toby has noticed that the Widow seems fascinated by the history and circumstances of his wound, and at first he is only too pleased to show her the very spot (on the map) where he got it. But she asks after it so frequently, so tenderly, that Toby is led to ascribe it to 'the compassionate turn and singular humanity of her character' (Vol. 9, Ch. 31, p. 801/p. 535). Trim gives a short cough on hearing this, but for the moment says no more. Does Bridget ask after the wound on your knee? asks Toby: no . . . says Trim. That shows, says Toby, in modest triumph, the difference between the two women. God bless your honour! cries Trim, why should Bridget be bothered about my *knee*?—which is so far from any place of real interest or concern—?

> My uncle Toby gave a long whistle——but in a note which could scarce be heard across the table.
> The Corporal had advanced too far to retire——in three words he told the rest——
> My uncle Toby laid down his pipe as gently upon the fender, as if it had been spun from the unravellings of a spider's web——
> ——Let us go to my brother Shandy's, said he. (Vol. 9, Ch. 31, p. 803/p. 536)

It would be tactless to inquire whether Toby has learnt more about the character of Woman or of himself through this, or indeed more about Trim. The Widow's concupiscence, Toby's modesty, Trim's knowledge of the way each has been working out of sight of the other, all are soundlessly revealed. Trim frees Toby, though not in the sense that Trim meant when he and Toby were at cross-purposes in Chapter 4, having their conversation about liberty. Trim flourishes his stick: 'Whilst a man is free—' (Vol. 9, Ch. 4, p. 743/p. 490) he cries, thinking about the Inquisition while Toby is thinking about the Widow's house and his own bowling-green and thus demonstrating once again his characteristic confinement in the resolute privacy of his own mind. But in the later chapter it is not just a question of his mind but also of his character or nature. His freedom lies in his being allowed to see that the Widow does not express his nature, while the bowling-green does. In this way he, like Tristram and Walter, learns something about the real relations between his own character and those of others, and so makes his entrance into the world. As with the episode with Walter in Chapter 1, the slightness of the stimuli is stressed: instead of the tap, a mere 'three words'. Not that such slight stimuli always achieve what Trim's words do; when Yorick spoke not three but five words 'point blank to the heart' (Vol. 4, Ch. 26, p. 377/p. 254), Toby's response was perfectly automatic. It is as much the delicacy, the unspokenness of the three words; and the 'spider's web' again recalls the 'dust of a butterfly's wing', the lightness of Mrs. Shandy's touch at a critical moment.

There remains the question of the wider kinds of liberty, social and political, which might seem to have been ignored. In fact all wider liberties depend, in *Tristram Shandy*, on the sense of personal liberty or personal identity; to allow that someone has a soul is to admit that they are in essence your equal. This point emerges in Chapter 6, in the course of Trim's narrative about the sausages and the Negro girl who flaps the flies away with a fly-whisk. Toby and Trim discuss her nature (compassionate) and her situation (persecuted). The crux of the discussion is not the social nature of her persecution, but whether or not a Negro has a soul. Toby and Trim agree in the affirmative. 'Why then . . . is a black wench to be used worse

than a white one?' (Vol. 9, Ch. 6, p. 748/p. 493). No idea, says
Toby. It's only because 'she has no-one to stand up for her'
says Trim. Quite, says Toby, and neither do her brethren; but
this is merely 'the fortune of war which has put the whip into
our hands *now*——where it may be hereafter, heaven
knows!——but be it where it will, the brave, Trim! will not
use it unkindly' (Vol. 9, Ch. 6, p. 748/p. 493). There is a
characteristically poignant touch of the ludicrous in Toby's
transformation of a real fly-whisk into the metaphorical whip
of colonial power, and in his rhetorical ascription of a whole
world of social relationship to two such casual powers as
'fortune' and man's better nature. In the real world, we feel,
social forces have more power, and man's better nature is not
free to be appealed to. But the episode does express the ironic,
understated and complex nature of the Shandean 'liberty',
which revolves to such a large extent around the recognition of
the ways in which the oddities of one's character interact with
the external world. Were *Tristram Shandy* a novel of the
subsequent generation, the 1790s or 1800s, these moments of
illumination would appear, suitably amplified, as critical
points in the hero's or heroine's emotional and social education, and as part of the narrative climax of the book. The scales
would fall from the young person's eyes as their previous
failings of conduct and perception were revealed to them, and
personal and social fulfilment would follow. Nothing so
romantic will ever happen at Shandy Hall; the ironic spirit of
the book means that the other, antagonistic, digressive pattern
must be allowed to repeat itself, in the final anecdote about the
parish bull. But on a wider scale, when the radical novelists of
the 1790s want to write a more social fiction, it is to the
philosophical tradition in which Sterne lies that they turn for
inspiration, rather than to the comparatively smug treatment
of Liberty that the eighteenth century's more popular poets
provided.[17]

Liberty in 'Tristram Shandy'

NOTES

1. John Traugott, *Tristram Shandy's World: Sterne's Philosophical Rhetoric* (Berkeley and Los Angeles: University of California Press, 1954), p. 120.
2. *The Clockmakers' Outcry against the Author of the Life and Opinions of Tristram Shandy* (1760), p. 11.
3. *A Letter from the Rev. George Whitefield, B.A., to the Rev. Laurence Sterne, the supposed author of a book entitled 'The Life and Opinions of Tristram Shandy, Gentleman'* (1760), p. 16.
4. *The Clockmakers' Outcry*, p. 11.
5. *A Supplement to the Life and Opinions of Tristram Shandy, Gent., Serving to Elucidate that work* (1760), p. 38. The three pamphlets, *The Clockmakers' Outcry, A Letter from . . . George Whitefield* and *A Supplement* are reproduced in *The Life and Times of Seven Major British Writers: Sterneiana* (New York: Garland), Vols. III, iii (1975), V, ii (1975) and IV, ii (1974) respectively.
6. *A Supplement to . . . Tristram Shandy*, pp. 80–1.
7. Ibid., p. 83.
8. Richard Barton, *Farrago, or, Miscellanies in Verse and Prose* (1739), pp. 180–81.
9. See *Letters*, pp. 304–7, for the 1767 letter in which Sterne tells Eliza Draper about Lord Bathurst's complimentary remarks to him, on how he was worthy of the memory of 'Addison, Steele, Pope, Swift, Prior—geniuses of that cast'.
10. Matthew Prior, *Alma; or, The Progress of the Mind* (1718), II, 222–24, 226–28, 238–40. *Works of Matthew Prior*, ed. H. Bunker Wright and Monroe K. Spears (Oxford: Clarendon Press, 1959), I, p. 306.
11. Ibid., II, 243–48. *Works*, I, p. 491.
12. Ibid., III, 302–5. *Works*, I, p. 503.
13. Helene Moglen, *The Philosophical Irony of Laurence Sterne* (Gainsville: University of Florida Press, 1975), p. 2.
14. Traugott, *Tristram Shandy's World*, pp. 43, 42.
15. Eric Rothstein, *Systems of Order and Inquiry in Later Eighteenth-Century Fiction* (Berkeley and Los Angeles: University of California Press, 1975), p. 77.
16. Ibid., p. 76.
17. See Gary Kelly, 'Intellectual Physicks', *Etudes Anglaises*, XXI (1978), pp. 161–75, for a study of the ways in which the radical novelists of the 1790s explore and develop the sociological ramifications of philosophical 'necessity'.

10

At this Moment in Space: Time, Space and Values in *Tristram Shandy*

by K. G. SIMPSON

Throughout *Tristram Shandy* Sterne's 'small HERO' rejects rules and defies authority. Harshly played upon as he is by a whimsical Fate, he may be pardoned for feeling that he suffers an excess of constraints by merely being, and can well do without being further limited by man-made regulations. The attack which Sterne mounts, via Tristram's account of his life and opinions, on intellectual authority functions on two levels: slavish reverence for learning is satirized by being taken to absurd lengths by Walter Shandy, the retired merchant and devout seeker after truth, who will scratch out a letter of Erasmus's dialogue on the advantages of a long nose in order to make the sense more worthy of that great thinker; but the book is also a profound, and riotously comic, critique of rationalism (which, Sterne makes it plain, is in his view anti-life) and associationism (the full implications of which are demonstrated by means of comic examples). While rejecting rationalism and neo-classicism as imposing, each in its own way, degrees of authority and systematization that are anti-individualistic, Sterne foresees Romantic individualism (to which empiricism and associationism were contributing much) and also identifies its limitations.

Tristram's account takes the form that it does because he represents Sterne's comic exemplification of Locke's view of identity. At the start of *An Essay Concerning Human Understanding* Locke denies the existence of innate ideas such as eternity or identity. At birth the mind is empty and, according to Locke,

> the senses at first let in particular ideas, and furnish the yet empty cabinet: and the mind by degrees growing familiar with some of them, they are lodged in the memory and names got to them. Afterwards the mind, proceeding farther, abstracts them, and by degrees learns the use of general names. In this manner the mind comes to be furnished with ideas and language.[1]

Especially noteworthy here is the primacy afforded to sensations; it is by sensations that the mind is furnished. Locke's view of identity then develops as follows:

> For since consciousness always accompanies thinking, and it is that that makes everyone to be what he calls 'self', and thereby distinguishes himself from all other thinking things; in this alone consists personal identity, i.e. the sameness of a rational being: and as far as this consciousness can be extended backwards to any past action or thought, so far reaches the identity of that person; it is the same self now it was then; and it is by the same self with this present one that now reflects on it, that that action was done.[2]

This view of identity has important implications when applied to fictional practice by Sterne in a spirit that reveals him as both interested and ready to be amused. It is tempting, but also unjust, to claim that Sterne rejects associationism outright by means of *reductio ad absurdum*. Rather, he endorses the associationist view but demonstrates in a comic fashion his awareness of its implicit dangers.

Sterne's attitude to the human condition, in which identity derives so much from the nature of associations, is ambivalent; we are both characterized and limited by the activities of our minds. Each of us evinces distinct patterns of association, and we all experience and exemplify the limitations of association (as Mrs. Shandy does). Sterne recognizes the validity, indeed the inevitability, of the individual response (in the words of Tristram, 'every man will speak of the fair as his own market has gone in it' (Vol. 1, Ch. 5, p. 8/p. 10)). In this Sterne reflects, and proceeds to demonstrate, in a comic manner, one of the central tenets of empiricism: abandon absolute, general, or normative criteria and any response may be held to be valid since it applies only to the individual concerned. Hume, for instance, had said that 'a thousand different sentiments, excited by the same object, are all right; because no sentiment represents what is really in the object.'[3] In an age dominated by objective science, empiricism both encouraged and endorsed idiosyncratic experience. How to reconcile aberrations of the individual mind to the harmonious order of nature is, as Ernest Tuveson notes, 'one of the problems of the age and underlies Shandyism'.[4] In Tristram's account of the variety of reactions to the news of Bobby's death (Vol. 5, Ch. 7) Sterne offers comic exemplification of subjectivity of response, and at the same time he reveals the ambivalence of his attitude; he asserts our right to be ourselves, and shows that in so doing we are both comically limited and worthy of compassion. Associationism by its very nature promotes such subjective relativism of response.

Applied to the writing of the novel, this means that Tristram can do anything that is consistent with his highly whimsical personality. By virtue of the free flux of the consciousness he can range 'backwards and forwards' through time in what he terms 'this rhapsodical work' (Vol. 1, Ch. 13, p. 39/p. 31). The logic of this particular case (to use Henry James's terms) is the logic of a distinctive consciousness which takes some pleasure in declaring 'I do all things out of all rule' (Vol. 4, Ch. 10, p. 337/p. 225). The trouble is that 'author' and 'authority', just as they are linked etymologically, were regarded as being inseparable. In being asked to be an author, Tristram is being required to engage in an activity which is inimical to his nature. Tristram finds it difficult to be authoritative about anything. As Lockean man, he offers a narrative which follows the sequence of his associations, and in the flux of the consciousness it is impossible to achieve that staticity which is conventionally inseparable from authority: hence the nature of Tristram's book. All of this suggests that, in his use of Tristram, Sterne anticipates and realizes the aim of the Modernist novelists (one thinks most readily of Virginia

Woolf) to create the illusion of tentativeness, unwillingness to judge, and absence of authorial authority. It suggests, too, that there is much in Sterne's novel to be identified in terms of recent work—and of much later writers—on the relationships between temporality and spatiality in fiction.

Through Tristram's account of his experiences Sterne shows life to be significant in terms of conception, birth and death, with everything between these existing in a state of flux. The incontestable 'facts' of life are birth, death and the constancy of the mind. Beyond these, any attempts at fixity or authoritative statement are futile since they will be rendered redundant or invalid by the subsequent flux of experience. Claims for authority are false: hence the sustained attack on learned authorities. Everything is shown to be relative to its point of occurrence in the flux of experience.

This has important effects in terms of Sterne's rendering of character. In the main he eschews physical description. Sterne never has Tristram depict Toby physically, for instance, but leaves us to visualize him (the point is made explicitly when a space is left in which the reader may draw the widow Wadman). What is essential in Sterne's view is that the reader should have knowledge of the character's mind. Since for Sterne it is the movement of the consciousness through past and present experience that largely constitutes individual identity, the novelist must render that consciousness in order to present a credible character. This means, in addition, that Sterne rejects emotional fixity and the sustaining of any emotional note as being false to the nature of experience. For Sterne emotions are complex or, if they are single, they rarely endure for long. Thus comic and tragic are inextricably mixed throughout the book. Perhaps the most poignant expression of Tristram's awareness of mortality is this:

> I will not argue the matter: Time wastes too fast: every letter I
> trace tells me with what rapidity Life follows my pen; the days
> and hours of it, more precious, my dear Jenny! than the rubies
> about thy neck, are flying over our heads like light clouds of a
> windy day, never to return more—everything presses on—
> whilst thou art twisting that lock,—see! it grows grey; and
> every time I kiss thy hand to bid adieu, and every absence

which follows it, are preludes to that eternal separation which
we are shortly to make.—
   —Heaven have mercy upon us both! (Vol. 9, Ch. 9, p. 754/
   p. 498)

This immediately gives way to the joking defiance of 'Now, for
what the world thinks of that ejaculation—I would not give a
groat.' For the complex being that Sterne perceives man to be,
no mood can endure. Once struck, a note is caught up in the
flux of experience and new experiences make it rapidly
redundant.

'There is nothing unmixt in this world'[5]: Sterne recognizes
emotional complexity and emotional flux as ineluctable, but
also worthy, aspects of the human condition. He has Tristram
speak for him when he exclaims 'Now I love you for this—and
'tis this delicious mixture within you which makes you dear
creatures what you are' (Vol. 5, Ch. 9, p. 435/p. 292). And he
has Tristram demonstrate it in that he can joke about
personally painful experience, such as the unexpected circumcision, and in that he manifests the fluidity of his own
emotions, however extreme. The encounter with 'poor Maria'
is a case in point. Tristram recognizes that contemplation of
the subject of Toby's amours has occasioned the following
mood:

> I was in the most perfect state of bounty and goodwill; and felt
> the kindliest harmony vibrating within me, with every
> oscillation of the chaise alike; so that whether the roads were
> rough or smooth, it made no difference; everything I saw, or
> had to do with, touched upon some secret spring either of
> sentiment or rapture. (Vol. 9, The Invocation, p. 781/p. 522)

Having got a hold, sentiment colours his every response, and
not least his reaction to 'poor Maria'. That sentiment should
be able to hold sway to this extent is unnatural, according to
Sterne, and he makes this plain from the account of Tristram's
situation and behaviour:

> As the postillion spoke this, MARIA made a cadence so
> melancholy, so tender and querulous, that I sprung out of the
> chaise to help her, and found myself sitting betwixt her and her
> goat before I relapsed from my enthusiasm.
>   MARIA looked wistfully for some time at me, and then at her

goat—and then at me—and then at her goat again, and so on, alternately—
—Well, Maria, said I softly—What resemblance do you find? (p. 783/p. 523)

By means of comedy Sterne warns against such polarization and prolongation of emotion as being self-indulgent and false to nature. 'True Shandeism . . . opens the heart and lungs' to the fact of emotional complexity and emotional fluidity.[6] This Tristram exemplifies when he concludes his account of his meeting with Maria on a quite different note: 'What an excellent inn at Moulins!'

The reader, too, is called into service to exemplify the same point. Tristram feigns extremes of Naturalism in having his prose mirror the last minutes of Le Fever as follows:

Nature instantly ebbed again,—the film returned to its place,—the pulse fluttered,—stopp'd—went on—throb'd—stopp'd again—moved—stopp'd—shall I go on?—No. (Vol. 6, Ch. 10, p. 513/p. 343)

The reader's response reflects his desire that the account and the emotional note be protracted no further.

The mistrust of the definitive includes, as Sterne shows through the example of Tristram, the individual's sense of identity. Here, too, attempts at fixity or authoritative statement are shown to be equally futile. Lionel Trilling, writing of Jane Austen's *Emma*, has claimed thus that uncertainty about self is a characteristic of the modern:

[Jane Austen] was aware of the increase of the psychological burden of the individual, she understood the new necessity of conscious self-definition and self-criticism, the need to make private judgements of reality. And there is no reality about which the modern person is more uncertain and more anxious than the reality of himself.[7]

If this is so Tristram is undeniably modern, as this encounter indicates:

It was a commissary sent to me from the post office, with a rescript in his hand for the payment of some six livres odd sous.
Upon what account? said I.—'Tis upon the part of the king, replied the commissary, heaving up both his shoulders—

Laurence Sterne: Riddles and Mysteries

—My good friend, quoth I,—as sure as I am I—and you are you—
    —And who are you? said he.——Don't puzzle me, said I. (Vol. 7, Ch. 33, p. 633/p. 421)[8]

If one adheres to the associationist thesis, then Tristram's uncertainty about his identity is quite true to life. Seen in this light, too, Tristram's habitual dialogues with the reader are more than an idiosyncrasy of personality; they are central to his quest for some means by which he can identify himself, some recurrent situations which he can control and in which he can relate to others by virtue of the degree of fixity inherent in those situations. They are of little avail, however (especially on those occasions where Tristram is offered contradictory advice by different readers), and the predominant sense is of the fluidity of experience which disrupts any definitive concept of identity. Biographical details are illuminating here. In Sterne's *Memoirs* is the revealing entry: 'In the year 1719 all unhing'd again'.[9] Is it possible that there is a relationship between the instability of Sterne's early life and his prose style, which habitually mirrors a mind in flux (endorsing his claim, 'Great wits jump')?

Pursued by Death, Tristram tries to keep several paces ahead of him. Troubled by the problems of authorship, he is torn between being himself and communicating something to his readers, which necessarily involves attaining to a measure of fixity. Through his choice of narrator and narrative technique Sterne makes a bold attempt to free the novel from the shackles of temporality. As Tristram flies defiantly in the face of death, so Sterne tries to free experience from the control of the temporal and liberate it into the realms of the spatial. It is a splendid paradox; Tristram, haunted by mortality and with his novel at the mercy of his whimsical consciousness, is the means whereby his creator transcends the temporal and achieves the fixity of the spatial. Volume 7 is largely concerned with Tristram's flight from death around Europe. Here is Chapter 28 in which Tristram experiences the co-presence of events:

Now this is the most puzzled skein of all—for in this last chapter, as far at least as it has helped me through *Auxerre*, I

have been getting forwards in two different journies together,
and with the same dash of the pen—for I have got entirely out
of Auxerre in this journey which I am writing now, and I am
got halfway out of Auxerre in that which I shall write hereafter—. There is but a certain degree of perfection in every
thing; and by pushing at something beyond that, I have
brought myself into such a situation as no traveller ever stood
before me; for I am this moment walking across the market
place of Auxerre with my father and my uncle Toby, in our
way back to dinner—and I am this moment also entering
Lyons with my post chaise broke into a thousand pieces—and
I am moreover this moment in a handsome pavillion built by
Pringello, upon the banks of the Garonne, which Mons.
Sligniac has lent me, and where I now sit rhapsodizing all
these affairs.

    —Let me collect myself, and pursue my journey. (Vol. 7,
Ch. 28, pp. 621–22/pp. 413–14)

In a brilliantly funny way Sterne here anticipates Proustian
simultaneity of experience and Jungian 'synchronicity', but
there is a dimension here that is distinctly his, because, in
addition, he is able to communicate to the reader his concern
with the relationships between, and possible incompatibility
of, experience and the literary rendering of it, his awareness of
the gap between the nature of the subject-matter and the
nature of the expressive medium.

Western culture is characterized by individualism and time-
sense, whereas Eastern culture stresses collectivism, the universal, and the a-temporal. Well in advance of those great
twentieth-century names that are associated with the subject,
Sterne recognized that Western culture is obsessed with the
time-dimension. Sterne identified and exploited the link in the
European rationalist tradition between consecutive and logical
reasoning (and its verbal expression) and chronology.

Quite rightly, Miriam Allott pointed out that Locke (deriving
much from Descartes) is largely responsible for influencing the
growth of 'a concept of individuality [that] is dependent on
particularity of place and time, and it is this precise spatial and
temporal location of individual experience which is really the
novel aspect of fiction.'[10] Sterne adapts this to his own purposes;
what he renders is individuality yearning after universality.
W. Jackson Bate observed that empiricism, 'in its opposition to

the universal, and in its emphasis on sensory and experiential proof, is also essentially anti-rationalistic' (and he notes that the result may be 'sceptical relativism').[11]

Through Tristram's attempt at relating his life and opinions Sterne makes it plain that experience is complex, sensations are simultaneous and often hybrid, and the pace of the mind's movement is variable. Yet he achieves all of this by means of a narrator who (quite apart from being a time-bound mortal) is trapped within the chronology of language:

> My mother, you must know,—but I have fifty things more necessary to let you know first;—I have a hundred difficulties which I have promised to clear up, and a thousand distresses and domestic misadventures crouding in upon me thick and three-fold, one upon the neck of another;—a cow broke in (to-morrow morning) to my uncle *Toby's* fortifications, and eat up two rations and a half of dried grass, tearing up the sods with it which faces his hornwork and covered way.—*Trim* insists upon being tried by a court-martial,—the cow to be shot,—*Slop* to be *crucifix'd*,—myself to be *tristram'd*, and at my very baptism made a martyr of;—poor unhappy devils that we all are!—I want swaddling,—but there is no time to be lost in exclamations.—I have left my father lying across his bed, and my uncle *Toby* in his old fringed chair, sitting beside him, and promised I would go back to them in half an hour, and five-and-thirty minutes are laps'd already.—(Vol. 3, Ch. 38, p. 278/p. 187)

By means of Tristram's comic plight Sterne shows that the complexity of experience cannot be rendered through the limited medium of language, but he also suggests that communication, unlike language, need not be time-bound; in place of the time-language co-ordinates he suggests the possibilities for communication in the relationship of spatiality and silence, thus anticipating the thinking of, among others, Proust and Beckett.

Much that has been written on the spatial-temporal dimension in literature is strikingly apposite to Sterne. One of the seminal works in this area was Joseph Frank's profound essay, 'Spatial Form in Modern Literature'. Frank stressed the importance of Lessing's *Laocoön*, not because of its innate validity, but because of the direction in which it pointed. There Lessing attacked pictorial poetry and allegorical painting because they were incompatible with the following principles (as described by Frank):

> Form in the plastic arts, according to Lessing, is necessarily spatial because the visible aspect of objects can best be presented juxtaposed in an instant of time. Literature, on the other hand, makes use of language, composed of a succession of words proceeding through time; and it follows that literary form, to harmonize with the essential quality of its medium, must be based primarily on some form of narrative sequence.[12]

Now in *Tristram Shandy* the sequence is primarily that of the conduct of the narrative, not the sequence that is inherent within the subject-matter that is narrated.

Lessing's *Laocoön* (1766) offered, according to Frank, 'a new approach to aesthetic form',[13] and what especially links it with Sterne is Lessing's attack on neo-classicism. While Lessing believed that the Greeks (in Joseph Frank's words) 'respected the limits imposed on different art mediums by the conditions of human perception', the effect of neo-classical regulation was that 'the form of a work was nothing but the technical arrangement dictated by the rules.'[14] Here, then, is the importance of Lessing's work, as Frank sees it in terms which indicate a clear affinity of spirit between Lessing and Sterne:

> For Lessing . . . aesthetic form is not an external arrangement provided by a set of traditional rules. Rather, it is the relation between the sensuous nature of the art medium and the conditions of human perception. The 'natural man' of the eighteenth century was not to be bound by traditional political forms but was to create them in accordance with his own nature. Similarly, art was to create its own forms out of itself rather than accept them ready-made from the practice of the past; and criticism, instead of prescribing rules for art, was to explore the necessary laws by which art governs itself. No longer was aesthetic form confused with mere externals of technique or felt as a strait jacket into which the artist, willy-nilly, had to force his creative ideas. Form issued spontaneously from the organization of the art work as it presented itself to perception. Time and space were the two extremes defining the limits of literature and the plastic arts in their relation to sensuous perception; and, following Lessing's example, it is possible to trace the evolution of art forms by their oscillations between these two poles.[15]

151

Frank proceeds to apply Lessing's method to modern literature and finds Eliot, Pound, Proust, and Joyce moving in the direction of spatial form. He observes:

> All of these writers intend the reader to apprehend their work spatially, in a moment of time, rather than as a sequence. And since changes in aesthetic form always involve major changes in the sensibility of a particular cultural period, an effort will be made to outline the spiritual attitudes that have led to the predominance of spatial form.[16]

In this context identification of Sterne in terms of *Zeitgeist* is rewarding. For long a considerable body of critical opinion regarded *Tristram Shandy* as at best whimsical and at worst perverse, but it is less than just to try to explain the book away in terms of the recesses of Sterne's personality. It is not simply the case that Sterne, by virtue of idiosyncrasies of temperament, is opposed to a great deal, if not anti-everything. Rather, his book has to be located in that crucial stage in the development of ideas when rationalism and neo-classicism were crumbling in the face of empiricism and individualism. On its every page *Tristram Shandy* speaks of individualism. But Sterne's movement towards spatiality is directly related to his awareness of the shortcomings of individualism; the world of self is the world of temporality and flux and the individual aspires to escape it into the fixity of the world of space.

Instrumental to such an attempt is, by virtue of its nature, the image. For Ezra Pound, 'an "Image" is that which presents an intellectual-emotional complex in an instant of time.'[17] The implications of this Joseph Frank sees to be these:

> an image is defined not as a pictorial reproduction but as a unification of disparate ideas and emotions into a complex presented spatially in an instant of time. Such a complex does not proceed discursively, in unison with the laws of language, but strikes the reader's sensibility with an instantaneous impact.[18]

Perhaps it is claiming too much to suggest that *Tristram Shandy* may be regarded as an extended image, but in every other respect what Frank says here may be applied to Sterne's novel. Tristram's attempt to write his book serves as metaphor for Sterne's world-view. By means of the narrative function of

Tristram's consciousness Sterne represents 'a unification of disparate ideas and emotions into a complex presented spatially'. Paradoxically, it is by means of the flux of Tristram's consciousness that Sterne clearly relates emotional complexity to spatiality (Tristram's emotions rarely appear singly; if they do, they soon give way to another, often their opposite).

'Everything should sound simultaneously',[19] remarked Flaubert of the county-fair scene in *Madame Bovary*. Taking this scene as an instance of the spatialization of form in the novel, Joseph Frank comments,

> For the duration of the scene, at least, the time-flow of the narrative is halted; attention is fixed on the interplay of relationships within the immobilized time-area. These relationships are juxtaposed independently of the progress of the narrative, and the full significance of the scene is given only by the reflexive relations among the units of meaning.[20]

This is exemplified by *Tristram Shandy*. The primary level of 'scene' in *Tristram Shandy* is that of the business of narration, with what is narrated comprising secondary 'scene'. In that area of primary 'scene' 'attention is fixed on the interplay of relationships within the immobilized time-area', and the full significance is apprehended only in terms of reflexive reference. 'I think' says Toby in Chapter 21 of Volume 1, and it is not until Chapter 6 of Volume 2 that Tristram gets round to recording the rest of the sentence. In Chapter 27 of Volume 3 Walter learns of the crushing of his son's nose and retires to his room. There he remains, referred to intermittently and attended by the sympathetic Toby, until Chapter 3 of Volume 4 when he breaks the silence with—unfortunately for him—a metaphor. Likewise, later, Mrs. Shandy is left eavesdropping while Tristram gets on with writing eight chapters (Vol. 5, Chs. 5–13). It is a striking paradox; the apparent author's terrible problems with temporality are the means whereby the actual author attains to spatiality.

This means the demise of the conventional plot, which is inseparably involved with temporality and the sequential or, generally, consequential organization of material. In a distinguished sequel to the work of Frank, Ivo Vidan has proposed that Ingarden's analysis of the way in which the work of literature is apprehended as knowledge by the reader may be employed to illuminate the communication of meaning in spatial fiction. 'The work', suggests Vidan, 'allows itself to be surveyed from many individual angles: what remains in the mind is always a condensed *Gestalt* rather than a book or a complete part of the book that has been perused.'[21] For the comprehension of book in terms of understanding of plot, substitute *gestalt*; and in this movement Sterne's novel has fulfilled a seminal function.

The use of Tristram's consciousness as centre of narration is one means by which Sterne achieves spatiality; another is the presence of reflexive reference. Reflexive reference in *Tristram Shandy* derives largely from the fact that the idiosyncrasies of personality and—particularly—of speech of both characters and narrator assume almost a personal mythopoeic dimension. Tristram lamenting the cough he got skating into the wind in Flanders, mentioning 'dear Jenny', or entreating the readers 'an' please your Worships'; Toby whistling Lillabullero, or exclaiming 'What prodigious armies we had in Flanders!'; Walter ever on the alert for the personal excruciation of the squeaking parlour-door hinge: these and many other traits of speech and behaviour recur, to the extent that they become motifs or (to think spatially) key-stones in the structure which is *Tristram Shandy*. One of the features that distinguishes Sterne's novel is the extent to which the motifs originate within the characters themselves, whereas most of the great spatial novels of the twentieth century are parasitic on the myths of classical, and more recent, literature (one need look no further than *Ulysses*, *To the Lighthouse*, and *Under the Volcano*).

The individual mythopoeic capacity of Sterne's characters is a manifestation of the hobby-horse. From the range of examples in *Tristram Shandy* it would appear that for Sterne the hobby-horse is a value-system which originates within the individual and which the individual will inevitably create. (Says Tristram, 'there is no disputing against HOBBY-HORSES; and, for my part, I seldom do. . . . Be it known . . . that I keep of couple of pads myself' (Vol. 1, Ch. 8, p. 12/ p. 13). Walter's dogged pursuit of Truth down the more arcane corridors of learning; Toby's re-creation of battles in miniature; Tristram's attempts (like everything else, against

all the odds) to relate his life and opinions; and, being conditioned by the nature of the vast majority of novels, the
reader's persistent attempt to read *Tristram Shandy* like a conventional novel: each of these is a hobby-horse. Tristram's
compassionate comments as follows on the effects of his
father's hobby-horsicality will do very well for Sterne on the
subject of man:

> ——Certainly it was ordained as a scourge upon the pride of
> human wisdom, That the wisest of us all should thus outwit
> ourselves, and eternally forego our purposes in the intemperate
> act of pursuing them. (Vol. 5, Ch. 16, p. 448/pp. 300–1)

At the heart of *Tristram Shandy* is a paradox, a paradox
which assumes several forms. It is the paradox of the mind,
forever in flux, expressing itself by means of structures. It is
the paradox of individualism, wherein the self, attaining to
freedom, finds itself limited either by exercising that freedom
or by finding itself in a void, and so longs for fixity. Empiricist
freedom, as Sterne depicts it, is a mixed blessing. Walter
Shandy, as his son tells us, 'would see nothing in the light in
which others placed it;—he placed things in his own light'
(Vol. 2, Ch. 19, p. 170/pp. 115–16). Walter is, simply, the
most extreme exemplar of what Sterne presents as the human
condition, in which freedom to respond or interpret invariably
reveals the limitations of individuality.

It is the paradox, too, of the relationship between the
associationist view of identity, in which the mind is in constant
flux, and the contribution of spatiality and fixity to the
expression of identity. *Tristram Shandy* has about it a clear effect
of movement, and it is a personal history of an attempt to
escape time. Having delayed the reader with the tale of the
Abbess of Andoüillets, Tristram exclaims in triumph, 'What a
tract of country have I run!—how many degrees nearer to the
warm sun am I advanced, and how many fair and goodly cities
have I seen, during the time you have been reading, and
reflecting, Madam, upon this story!' (Vol. 7, Ch. 26, p. 615/
p. 409). Such successes are rare, however. Chased by time,
Tristram tries to lose time in the spatiality of his account, but
he is repeatedly caught in the snares of authorial time. While
Tristram is time-bound, his experiences and the relation of

155

them are rendered permanent. So too is that Tristram who is characterized by his presence within the narrative. Chapter 20 of Volume 6 finds Tristram enjoining the reader to 'leave' a range of people that includes mother, Slop, and Le Fever, and culminates thus:

> —And last of all,—because the hardest of all—Let us leave, if possible, *myself*:—But 'tis impossible,—I must go along with you to the end of the work. (Vol. 6, Ch. 20, p. 533–34/p. 355)

A narrative 'self' has been established and identified, and Tristram realizes this and longs to leave that very 'self'.

Tristram has been characterized in terms of his hobby-horse—the relating of his life and opinions. From Sterne's presentation of it, the limitations of the hobby-horse are plain; it is limited and limiting to an extent that renders the individual absurd, and in a world in which the consequences of actions seem far outwith the control of the doer (witness the succession of events that leads to the crushing of Tristram's nose, or that leading to his circumcision) such limitation reinforces that sense of fatalism to which Tristram himself gives frequent expression. As Sterne depicts life, actions seem immediately to acquire an existence independent of the doer, and a measure of life's chaos is the extent to which human actions have just such an autonomy. Despite all this, Sterne does seem to say that the hobby-horse is all we have. Given the impossibility of ordering life, the hobby-horse—the system or structure of values which the individual erects out of his personal contact with life, and which comes to be the means by which he is individualized—has the undeniable attraction of being constant, a ready rule-of-thumb. The hobby-horse, however absurd it renders the individual, is at least something to offer against the anarchy of life.

What Sterne does is to represent empiricist man, endowed with these various characteristics, and to suggest that he *is* universal. This may be one of the factors that led Edwin Muir to write of Toby and Walter: 'They are not figures of comedy in a picture of society, but naturals of humour in a world of universal forces.'[22] Tristram, Toby, Walter, the reader—each rides his hobby-horse and, in so doing, demonstrates how actuality and version of actuality will ever diverge.

This means that in *Tristram Shandy* technique and subject are one. The points which are exemplified by the characters in the action (subjectivity, hobby-horse, idiosyncratic association) are also substantiated by the technique of narration. Joseph Frank cites Wilhelm Worringer to the effect that, for a true psychology of style, the 'formal value' must be shown 'to be an accurate expression of the inner values in such a way that duality of form and content ceases to exist'.[23] This is exactly what Sterne accomplishes in *Tristram Shandy*. He renders what Vidan (writing of *Lord Jim* and *The Good Soldier*) terms 'the complex structure of relativity, the gradual subjectively directed revelation of fact'.[24] The fact that Sterne, by using an apparently incompetent and unauthoritative narrator, expressed all this clearly and definitively is perhaps both the ultimate paradox and the highest tribute to his achievement.

NOTES

1. John Locke, *E.C.H.U.*, Bk. I, Ch. 2, p. 55.
2. Ibid., Bk. II, Ch. 27, p. 335.
3. Cited Walter Jackson Bate, *From Classic to Romantic* (Cambridge, Mass.: Harvard University Press, 1946; repr. New York, 1961), p. 102.
4. Ernest Tuveson, 'Locke and the "Dissolution of the Ego"', *Modern Philology*, LII, (1954–55), 167.
5. *SJ*, p. 228.
6. Compare Diderot on his facial expressions: 'I had a hundred different ones a day, according to the mood that was on me. I was serene, sad, dreamy, tender, violent, passionate, eager. The outward signs of my many and varying states of mind chased one another so rapidly across my face that the painter's eye caught a different one from moment to moment, and never got me aright' (cited Paul Hazard, *European Thought in the Eighteenth Century* (Harmondsworth: Penguin Books, 1965), p. 408).
7. Lionel Trilling, *Beyond Culture* (Harmondsworth: Penguin Books, 1967), p. 54.
8. Compare *SJ*, p. 221: 'There is not a more perplexing affair in life to me, than to set about telling anyone who I am—for there is scarce anybody I cannot give a better account of than of myself; and I have often wished I could do it in a single word—and have an end of it.'
9. *Letters*, p. 2.
10. Miriam Allott, *Novelists on the Novel* (London: Routledge & Kegan Paul, 1965), p. 181.
11. Bate, pp. 93–4.

12. Joseph Frank, *The Widening Gyre: Crisis and Mastery in Modern Literature* (New Brunswick, N.J.: Rutgers University Press, 1963), p. 6.
13. Ibid., p. 7.
14. Loc. cit.
15. Ibid., p. 8.
16. Ibid., p. 9.
17. Cited Frank, p. 9.
18. Loc. cit.
19. Gustave Flaubert, *Oeuvres Complètes* (Paris, 1947), 'Correspondence', III (1852–54), 75.
20. Frank, p. 15.
21. Ivo Vidan, 'Time Sequence in Spatial Fiction', *Studia Romanica et Anglica Zagrabiensia*, XXIII (1–2), 1978, 206.
22. Edwin Muir, 'Laurence Sterne', *Essays on Literature and Society* (London: Hogarth Press, 1965), p. 57.
23. Frank, p. 58. To the Formalists, who disclaimed any distinction between form and content, *Tristram Shandy* was a major text. In 'A Russian Critic and *Tristram Shandy*', *Modern Philology*, LII, (1954–55), 98, Kenneth E. Harper glosses Victor Shklovsky's view that 'Sterne's constant revelation of the formal laws of art is so pronounced that the content of this novel can be described only as the perception of its form', and he cites Shklovsky's comment that '*Tristram Shandy* is the most typical novel in world literature.'
24. Vidan, p. 215.

Part Four:

AFTERWORD

11

Sterne and the Formation of Jane Austen's Talent

by PARK HONAN

To observe how Sterne affected Jane Austen is really to see
Tristram Shandy and *A Sentimental Journey* in fresh light. How
shall we do this? To list 'echoes' of Sterne—or apparent
ones—in her own novels would be a barren exercise, as I fear
that it is to list Sternean borrowings in Dickens or Joyce.
Rather, let us try to keep in view just what the Austen
biographers tell us least about, the concatenation of circumstances and forces that caused Jane Austen's talent to develop
in artistically formative years of her life, say from 1789 to 1813,
or from the years of James and Henry Austen's St. John's
College weekly, *The Loiterer*, and her own 'Love and Freindship' when she was 13 and 14, to the year in which *Mansfield
Park* was finished and her first three novels were either in print
or virtually complete in manuscript, when she was 37. In these
two dozen years, Sterne's novels helped Jane Austen in three
ways: as Whiggish foils for her Toryism; as heuristic texts to
further her narrative experiments; and as *exempla* or models of
wit, jokes, the comedy of the commonplace, and an attitude to
language. Ezra Pound noticed the last point when he claimed
the link between Sterne, Crabbe, and Jane Austen was a
shared 'value' of 'writing words that conform precisely with
fact, of free speech without evasions and circumlocutions' and
added that they all used direct, fact-oriented styles to record
'states of consciousness that their verse-writing contemporaries

scamp', and did so with a delicacy we sense now and then in Prévost or Constant.[1]

But there is usually a strong attitude behind a brave, new view of prose style. In 1789 or 1790, in-between playing a Dibden air and working on the satin stitch, the younger daughter of a Tory rector in Hampshire surely did not say to herself, 'I will write like that nice Mr. Yorick.' The Whiggishness of Mr. Yorick made him seem *not nice at all*; 'Jane, when a girl, had strong political opinions' as her nephew wrote in his *Memoir*,[2] and her own pro-Stuart, pro-Catholic annotations in Goldsmith's *History of England*, her friendships with Mrs. Lefroy and Mrs. Knight (who admired Mary Queen of Scots), her own juvenile 'History of England' (1791) and loving admiration of her father and her brothers James and Henry, all ardent Tories, show us, besides other evidence, that Jane Austen in her youth detested Whiggery. Three early events in her life deepened her Toryism. First, her brothers James and Henry launched in 1789 at St. John's College their weekly periodical, *The Loiterer*, partly to strike at the Whigs of Oxford who had supported the American Revolution and the Whigs of London who were trying to circumscribe the powers of the Austens' beloved King George III. Second, as if to humiliate the Austens themselves, oratorical Whigs such as Sheridan and Burke put the Austens' friend and well-wisher and patron, Warren Hastings, on trial for 'high crimes and misdemeanours' and slandered him for seven years (1788–95) before he was cleared of charges fixed to his tenure as Governor-General of Bengal. Third, the Revolution of 1789, about which many Whigs had been soft (or, as we would say in the days of Mrs. Thatcher, 'wet'), led to *La Terreur*, which by 1794 had claimed Jane Austen's cousin Eliza's husband, the Comte de Feuillide, as one of its victims. Whiggery, in one form or another, struck savagely at the Austens of Steventon. So it is not surprising that Jane Austen struck back at that Whig, Mr. Yorick of *A Sentimental Journey*, in a key scene in her most profound novel at the end of our period under review. She opposed Laurence Sterne in a very interesting way.

One of her main points in *Mansfield Park* is that Sir Thomas Bertram and his lady have brought up their children so badly that the estate is undermined, and its moral decay is to be seen in Maria Bertram's adultery. What, but Mr. Yorick, has worked a way into Maria's vain, lightsome consciousness? Maria is engaged to Mr. Rushworth. On the famous visit to Sotherton, Maria and her future seducer Henry Crawford meet at a locked gate in the park. Beyond the gate, their sexual play may begin. 'The sun shines and the park looks very cheerful', says Maria to her willing seducer. 'But unluckily that iron gate, that ha-ha, give me a feeling of restraint and hardship. I cannot get out, as the starling said.'³

' "I can't get out—I can't get out," said the starling,' Sterne's Yorick had reported in *A Sentimental Journey* after fearing that as a passportless man in war-time France he may be locked up in 'the Bastile':——'And as for the Bastile! the terror is in the word.'⁴ Indeed, terror *was* in the word. *A Sentimental Journey* was published in 1768. Less than three decades later 'terror' had become a political word associated for the first time with ultimate solutions sought by sane men, and Jane Austen's cousin Eliza lost her husband to the guillotine of *La Terreur* in Paris. Yorick's starling led Yorick to a paean on unbridled 'LIBERTY', and so Jane Austen has Maria Bertram's reckless 'I cannot get out, as the starling said' point to the adultery that destroys Maria as a person. Jane Austen damns Sterne even further. Maria is oppressed by a 'feeling of restraint and hardship' which suggests necessary ingredients in education that Yorick, a 'LIBERTY'-monger, forgets; and so at the end of *Mansfield Park* Sir Thomas Bertram is redeemed only when he, as father and educator, belatedly knows the values 'of early hardship and discipline'.⁵ Since Maria was over-indulged, she is by then ruined and lost.

Yet Jane Austen's political and moral objections to Sterne did not keep her from knowing and liking his work and using him. She thought against her prejudices, which is to think two or three ways about a matter, and let herself be 'taken in' by the companionable humour, trivial and time-squandering details, and unrushed reports of moment-by-moment household circumstances in the daily and believable life of Shandy Hall. There is good evidence that she knew *Tristram Shandy* as minutely as the seven volumes of Richardson's *Sir Charles Grandison*, and expected her sister Cassandra to know *Shandy*

just as well. 'James is the delight of our lives,' she writes to
Cassy about a servant at Lyme, on 14 September 1804, 'he is
quite an uncle Toby's annuity to us.—My Mother's shoes
were never so well blacked before, & our plate never looked so
clean.'[6] That allusion supposes that her sister Cassy will recall
Uncle Toby's words in the twenty-second chapter of the third
volume, and the ensuing dialogue:

> —Have I not a hundred and twenty pounds a year, besides my
> half-pay? cried my uncle *Toby.*——What is that, replied my
> father, hastily,—to ten pounds for a pair of jack-boots?——
> twelve guineas for your *pontoons* . . .—these military operations
> of yours are above your strength . . .——dear *Toby*, they will in
> the end quite ruin your fortune, and make a beggar of you.——
> What signifies it if they do, brother, replied my uncle *Toby*, so
> long as we know 'tis for the good of the nation.—(Vol. 3,
> Ch. 22, p. 242/p. 163)

By 1804, Jane Austen's sailor brothers Frank and Charles
risked their lives 'for the good of the nation'; her brothers
James and Henry had risked their reputations at Oxford and
her cousin Eliza's godfather Hastings had risked his neck 'for
the good of the nation'. Jane Austen, who read works on the
British Empire and debated imperial policy with her brothers,
wrote deliberately for the Tory good of the nation. (Despite
the ignorance of many of her biographers, she was politically
well-informed, though her novels in showing the *home* effects of
war-time on young women of the gentry class are more than
Tory propaganda.) Why, then, had she absorbed Sterne?

Sterne's *Tristram Shandy* had seemed to her a clearing
operation, as well as a storehouse of jokes. It called her attention
to each uncritically accepted device of fiction. We have no
'chapters' in our real lives and so instead of mutely accepting
the device of 'chapters', Tristram highlights it. Even Parson
Yorick rides 'to the very end of the chapter' (Vol. 1, Ch. 10,
p. 22/p. 19). Jane Austen, as a girl, highlights and plays with
the 'chapter' device, too, and gets us to laugh at it, as in 'The
Beautifull Cassandra' written when she was 12 or 13:

CHAPTER THE 6th

Being returned to the same spot of the same Street she had sate
out from, the Coachman demanded his Pay.

CHAPTER THE 7th

She searched her pockets over again & again; but every search was unsuccesfull. No money could she find. The man grew peremptory. She placed her bonnet on his head & ran away.

CHAPTER THE 8th

Thro' many a street she then proceeded & met in none the least Adventure till on turning a Corner of Bloomsbury Square, she met Maria.

CHAPTER THE 9th

Cassandra started & Maria seemed surprised; they trembled, blushed, turned pale & passed each other in a mutual silence.[7]

One by one Tristram's devices that call attention to the fictiveness of fiction are aped. Jane offers a series of meaningless or ironic dedications in the Shandean vein. One sequence of her mad 'Morsels' is dedicated to a lady six *weeks* old, 'trusting you will in time be older'. Patrons are solicited. 'Madam,' Jane Austen addresses an aloof, important deity who shared her amusements, her own sister,

> You are a Phoenix. Your taste is refined, your Sentiments are noble, & your Virtues innumerable. Your Person is lovely, your Figure, elegant, & your Form, magestic. Your Manners are polished, your Conversation is rational & your appearance singular. If therefore the following Tale will afford one moment's amusement to you, every wish will be gratified of
> Your most obedient
> humble servant
> THE AUTHOR[8]

The merriment and flexible, witty tactics of Tristram become touchstones of the prose Jane Austen wants; she responds to Yorick, who has 'as much life and whim, and *gaité de coeur* about him, as the kindliest climate could have engendered and put together' (Vol. 1, Ch. 11, p. 27/p. 22), and indeed she reads (at about the age of 13) in Sterne that Yorick carries no ballast, is unpractised in the world, and knows 'just about as well how to steer his course in it, as a romping, unsuspicious girl of thirteen' (p. 28/p. 22). Almost all of Tristram's comments on his mother are condescending, and Jane Austen at least by the time of 'Lesley Castle' (in its seventh letter, written at age 16) is a critic of male attitudes; and indeed *Shandy* is valuable to her for its critical, probing catalogue of novelistic devices. By mocking these devices as in 'Love and Freindship' Jane Austen freed herself from slavishly imitating the worst faults of novels. And yet when she began serious comedy of her own in 'Catherine or The Bower', she failed.

She failed not so much because 'Kitty' is inconsistent, as because the author lacked a narrative voice. Here again Sterne was valuable to her because he had found a way of bridging between a cold text and its readers. The point of the 'digressions' in *Tristram Shandy*—that word is Tristram's own—is that they interrupt narrative to bring 'the reader' into the novel. (*Shandy* makes more of the reader than any other work of the century.) Politically the middle class in a century of lending libraries, newspapers, journals and bourgeois revolutions cried out its importance, and *Shandy* is Whiggish in its digressions which admit 'the reader' into the text. The Shandean narrator is politically alert to his age. Jane Austen's narrator is the last element of her art that she developed. She avoided the problem in cold, uncertain works such as 'Lady Susan' and perhaps in epistolary drafts called 'Elinor and Marianne', 'First Impressions' and 'Susan' (all of which are missing). 'Susan', later called 'Catherine' and still later called *Northanger Abbey*, seems to have been her first lengthy work that reached a third-person narrative form; but we cannot assume that even this was not epistolary in early drafts. What we do know, as Henry Austen tells us, is that his sister's works were 'gradual performances', many times revised. One aim of the revisions, certainly, was to achieve in her narrator's voice an intimacy, authority and likeability close to that of Tristram's and Yorick's. In other words, she had to reach out to the reader, to bring the reader into her text in effect with the amiability of Sterne, and yet without any Whiggish overtones, since the comic Jane Austen was concerned to accompany her stories—and in a measure to interpret them—with a winning and morally certain Tory authority in her narrative persona. In the slow development of this personal voice, she was saved from gravity and pomposity partly by Sterne; indeed, she erred on the side of facetiousness, as we see from the opening chapters of *Northanger Abbey*, which we think is the least revised of her three early novels, and in which the narrator is on less comfortable terms with us than the narrators of *Pride and Prejudice* or even *Sense and Sensibility*. We must not overrate Sterne's importance to her, though. For moral authority she had the examples—and foils—of her brothers' *Loiterer* stories from which she learned lessons. It is hard to imagine that she was indifferent to the *Loiterer* story (we do not know which St. John's College friend of James Austen's wrote it) about the sad Scottish soldier who fought against Washington and was seduced by a democratic ideology, only to return to Scotland and lament that he had forgotten the 'pride' and 'prejudice' of his nation's monarchical ideals; this story was recited at Steventon rectory not later than 1790. Standing behind James and Henry Austen's *Loiterer* were Addison, Steele, Dr. Johnson, and the rich tradition of the moral periodical essay, which Mary Lascelles correctly assumes to be a mainstay of Jane Austen's art in its formation. But, we recall, she attacks *The Spectator* in *Northanger Abbey*; in that novel it is very clear she carries out a running debate with her most talented brother, James, who in his play-prefaces and epilogues and in an unpublished poem on his sister Jane Austen clarifies his (very logical) Tory opposition to novels of all kinds. So, we may say, she worked out her moral positions with the help of her family. She worked out the tone of her narrative voice with the help of Sterne.

But what is the essence of this tone, and how did Sterne's 'digressions' help the reviser of 'First Impressions' (composed between October 1796 and August 1797) and of 'Susan' (written in 1798–99 according to Cassandra Austen's note on the novel she describes as 'North-hanger Abbey')?[9] In *Tristram Shandy*, the 'digressions' are as functional as they are daring. They give the author special access to the reader; they keep the reader from swallowing a narrative unreflectingly, and they bring variety to *Shandy*'s discourse. But, as they substitute for 'story' and displace narrative, they in effect put Sterne out on a very thin high wire over the abyss of artistic failure. They *must* beguile and charm the reader first of all by means of a polished, very clear, seemingly casual, realistic style which has the warmth, wit and authenticity of Tristram's speaking voice. In no other novels available to her, not in Fielding, not in Defoe and Swift, not even in the finest sections of Burney's third-person *Camilla* (published 12 July 1796, and read before she reached Rowling House that summer by its subscriber Jane Austen, who learned much from this story about a Hampshire clergyman's second daughter named Camilla Tyrold), is there to be found a narrative voice so spontaneous, precise and humanly authentic as the voices of Tristram in *Shandy* and Yorick in *Sentimental Journey*. 'Digressions, incontestably, are the sunshine,' boasts Tristram, 'the life, the soul of reading' (Vol. 1, Ch. 22, p. 81/p. 58). But most digressors are bores, and Sterne's expert and painstakingly filed digressions hold the reader only because the tone of the prose style is perfect. It is their style that offers the reviser of 'First Impressions' her highest mark of style, and gives her an example of the casual, polished perfection of the speaking voice to match; and perhaps among British novelists only Jane Austen in her narrative voice, her most subtle and important achievement, can be ranked with Sterne. She did find models of concinnity and smart polish in Burney, as in this description of Mrs. Mittin, the former milliner, in *Camilla*:

> To be useful she would submit to any drudgery; to become agreeable, devoted herself to any flattery. To please was her incessant desire, and her rage for popularity included every rank and class of society.[10]

But that is lame, compared to this:

> *Her* mind was less difficult to develope. She was a woman of mean understanding, little information, and uncertain temper. When she was discontented she fancied herself nervous. The business of her life was to get her daughters married; its solace was visiting and news.[11]

We are not looking for *echoes* of Sterne here. Jane Austen's style is her own. What we say is that the authenticity of the rhythm, the casual perfection of the balances, and the unoppressive 'speaking' wit in the second example are achieved by a woman who knew *Tristram Shandy* as intimately as her Lyme letter of 1804 shows she did. It is the artistic daring of the Whiggish digressor, in Sterne, that is of value to Jane Austen as she fashions an omniscient voice of Tory moral authority; she could use Fanny Burney because she had studied the casual, accurate felicity of Sterne's prose style in the digressions.

She found in the digressions other lessons, too, only a few of which she could have found in Fielding, Charlotte Lennox, Charlotte Smith, Clara Reeve, Mrs. Inchbald, Jane West, or other novelists or *Lady's Magazine* (and other) periodical writers she studied. Tristram's digressions help to give life to his portraits of Walter Shandy, his wife, Uncle Toby, Trim, Mrs. Wadman and lesser figures. Tristram animates by changing perspective; he gives the touch of life by a withdrawal, a leaving of the created thing. We imagine, then, that what is sketched has its ongoing life; usually the digression has either a playful relevance to the character sketch that is dropped, or an allusion within it, a digression from the digression to remind us that an action in time waits for Tristram to get back to it. The slight awkwardness of some of the narrator-intrusions in *Northanger Abbey* may owe to Jane Austen's underestimation of the complexity of Sterne's digressive tactics. Later, she uses narrative comment, and less often generalization on a theme, with a subtlety that is as effective as Sterne's technique of animating a set of characters by withdrawing his narrator from their presence. By changing her narrative mode, furthermore, Jane Austen appeals to the reader's judgement and feelings alike; she establishes her narrator's intense and sensible moral authority; and, when we have made every allowance for the difference between her own Toryism and Sterne's mild Whiggery, we see, as we should expect to see, beneath political levels of meaning in their books, a world-view that is only slightly dissimilar in Sterne and Austen. Sterne's deepest theme is death or evanescence; Jane Austen's deepest theme is happiness, with death-of-spirit as its adversary. Sterne would divert us *not* from the thought of final things, or Christian teleology, but from gloom or morbidity by appealing comically to the feelings; he is a very unusual, unsaccharine sentimentalist. Jane Austen narrowly saves her Marianne from physical death, and saves all of her heroines from a Maria Rushworth-like death-of-spirit by having them struggle to preserve their full capacity to feel. The test of a heroine's liveliness, life-of-spirit, is always in her real *sense* and *sensibility*, favourable words for the author as they involve perception, feeling and intellect. Anne Elliott has 'strong' sensibility and Henry Tilney 'real' sensibility since they accurately perceive feeling in others; 'excessive' or 'false' sensibility as long as it lasts, as in Marianne Dashwood's case, prevents just that heightened perception of feeling.[12]

Hence Jane Austen is, like Sterne, another realistic, unsaccharine sentimentalist to the extent that an attitude to *feeling* is at the centre of her psychology of perception and her view of human relationships. She could respond deeply to Sterne, the wry, comic, innovating, rule-breaking sentimentalist. His serious delight in lexical games, riddles, word-play and word meanings appealed to her after she left off writing *jeux d'esprit* stories and began the hard task of forming her narrative voice; in *Emma*, and elsewhere, Sternean riddles and word-play are her tools. He rolled out a comic world for her. He used a subtle, flexible prose style to interpret it. And if not in *Mansfield Park*, at least in writing to her beloved sister she could forgive him for his Whiggish moral laxity.

NOTES

1. 'How to Read' and 'The Rev. G. Crabbe, LL.B.', in *Literary Essays of Ezra Pound*, ed. T. S. Eliot (London: Faber and Faber, 1968), pp. 31 and 276.
2. J. E. Austen Leigh, *A Memoir of Jane Austen*, 2nd edn. (London: Richard Bentley, 1871), p. 83.
3. Jane Austen, *Mansfield Park*, ed. R. W. Chapman (Oxford: Oxford University Press, 1923), p. 99.
4. *SJ*, pp. 196, 197.
5. *Mansfield Park*, p. 473.
6. *Jane Austen's Letters*, ed. R. W. Chapman, 2nd edn. (Oxford: Oxford University Press, 1979), p. 140. The holograph of this letter shows a dash before the word 'My'.
7. 'The Beautifull Cassandra, A Novel in Twelve Chapters', in Jane Austen, *Minor Works*, ed. R. W. Chapman, rev. edn. with notes by B. C. Southam (Oxford: Oxford University Press, 1980), pp. 45–6.
8. Ibid., p. 44.
9. See the photo-facsimile of Cassandra Austen's note in Jane Austen, *Minor Works*, facing p. 242.

10. Frances Burney, *Camilla or A Picture of Youth*, ed. Edward A. Bloom and Lillian D. Bloom (London: Oxford University Press, 1972), p. 688.
11. Jane Austen, *Pride and Prejudice*, ed. James Kinsley and Frank W. Bradbrook (Oxford: Oxford University Press, 1980), p. 3.
12. See the useful discussion of *sense* and *sensibility* in John Odmark, *An Understanding of Jane Austen's Novels: Character, Value and Ironic Perspective* (Oxford: Basil Blackwell, 1981), pp. 168–72.

Annotated Bibliography (1977–83)

by W. G. DAY

Early critical response to Sterne's works is considered by Alan B. Howes in *Yorick and the Critics: Sterne's Reputation in England, 1760–1868* (New Haven: Yale University Press, 1958; repr. Hamden, Conn.: Archon Books, 1971), and extracts covering the period 1759–1839 may be found in Howes's *Sterne: The Critical Heritage* (London: Routledge & Kegan Paul, 1974). Two annotated bibliographies by Lodwick Hartley cover the years 1900–77: *Laurence Sterne in the Twentieth Century* (Chapel Hill: University of North Carolina Press, 1966), and, *Laurence Sterne: An Annotated Bibliography, 1965–1977* (Boston, Mass.: G. K. Hall & Co., 1978). Hartley's works are not without omissions, and the index numbers are occasionally awry, but he does include the essential critical works of the period.

The following list covers only the years 1977–83 and is intended to be partial, both in bias and in content. It includes those works which I have read in the period and have found useful. Absence of any particular work does not necessarily mean that I have discarded it as wanting; with the ever-increasing volume of published Sterne studies it is becoming difficult to keep up, particularly with journals of limited circulation. (N.B. This bibliography is not covered by the index.)

I. Bibliographical Aids

1. MONKMAN, FRANCIS and KENNETH, *A Concordance to the Sermons of Sterne* (for availability write to: Kenneth Monkman, Shandy

Hall, Coxwold, York). A computer-generated concordance based upon the first editions of the seven volumes of sermons. A useful companion to the concordances of Graves and the Pastas to *Tristram Shandy* and *A Sentimental Journey*.

2. MONKMAN, KENNETH, 'Bibliographical Descriptions', Appendix Five, pp. 907–38 of item 4 below. Kenneth Monkman is the doyen of Sterne studies, particularly the bibliographic. This is an admirably clear account of the lifetime editions of *Tristram Shandy* and is essential reading for scholars, collectors and book-dealers. The next item adds an interesting qualification.

3. MONKMAN, KENNETH, '*Tristram* in Dublin', *Transactions of the Cambridge Bibliographical Society*, 7 (1979), 343–68. Eighteenth-century Dublin editions of literary texts have caused a number of bibliographical problems. In this article Kenneth Monkman produces what I consider to be incontrovertible evidence that Dodsley's edition of Volumes I and II of *Tristram Shandy*, so long believed to be the second edition after that of York, is the third or even the fourth edition, in that there is at least one edition (and possibly two) printed in Dublin by Chamberlaine and clearly antedating Dodsley.

II. Editions

4. *The Life and Opinions of Tristram Shandy, Gentleman: The Text*, ed. Melvyn and Joan New (Gainesville: University Presses of Florida, 1978), 2 vols. This text forms the first two volumes of the University of Florida edition of Sterne's *Works*. It is the first scholarly text based upon a collation of the early editions, is accurate down to such details as the lengths of the dashes, has been set up in a very readable format, and is the edition from which all scholarly references should be taken. There are extensive bibliographical appendices. The annotations are due to appear in September 1984.

5. *The Life and Opinions of Tristram Shandy, Gentleman*, ed. Howard Anderson (New York: W. H. Norton, 1980). Principally of interest because of the critical essays collected at the end of the book. One of the cheapest available editions.

6. ———, ed. Ian Campbell Ross (Oxford: Oxford University Press, 1983). The text is based upon first editions throughout, unlike the immediately preceding item. The introduction and notes have the air of having been written some time before publication.

III. Criticism

A. General

7. BONY, ALAIN, 'Terminologie chez Sterne', Poétique, 29 (1977), 28–49. A piece to be approached with some caution in that M. Bony bases his argument upon French translations of the two novels with the result that there are moments, as in Sainéan's *L'Influence et la Réputation de Rabelais* (Paris: Librairie Universitaire J. Gamber, 1930), where niceties of argument depend upon the translation rather than Sterne's original. The final word of footnote 27 should read '*hand*'.

8. CONRAD, PETER, *Shandyism: The Character of Romantic Irony* (Oxford: Basil Blackwell, 1978). Conrad starts with the observation: 'This is a book less about than around *Tristram Shandy*.' It deals with the influence of Sterne on the Romantics and is rather more illuminating about the latter than the former.

9. FREEDMAN, WILLIAM, *Laurence Sterne and the Origins of the Musical Novel* (Athens: University of Georgia Press, 1978). In the light of Sterne's references to music Freedman develops the idea and considers the whole of *Tristram Shandy* in terms of music. Reviewed cautiously by William Holtz in *Eighteenth-Century Studies*, 13 (1979–80), 112–15. I found Freedman's arguments interesting but evidently requiring more knowledge of music than I have.

10. LOVERIDGE, MARK, *Laurence Sterne and the Argument About Design* (London: Macmillan, 1982). An attempt to provide for *Tristram Shandy* what Martin Battestin did for *Tom Jones* in an article, '*Tom Jones*: The Argument of Design', in *The Augustan Milieu*, ed. H. K. Miller, E. Rothstein and G. S. Rousseau (Oxford: Oxford University Press, 1970), pp. 289–319. Traces ideas of design in the late seventeenth and early eighteenth century and pursues his argument in relation to Sterne by detailed analysis, most of which works well, but the section relating to uncle Toby's wound and Locke (pp. 131–35) is undermined by the repeated claim that Toby was 'struck by the cannonball'.

11. McGILCHRIST, IAIN, 'Sterne' in *Against Criticism* (London: Faber, 1982), pp. 131–75. Of critical pieces on Sterne, written in whatever age, this is one of the very few which I would nominate essential reading. This piece has style and ideas. Not to be missed.

12. ROHMANN, GERD (ed.), *Laurence Sterne* (Darmstadt: Wissenschaftliche Buchgesellschaft, 1980). The first two sections, in

German, attempt to assess Sterne's reputation between 1767 and 1864. These sections are followed by a collection of essays, principally in English, dating from 1909 to 1977, and including important pieces by Virginia Woolf, Work, Baird and Mayoux. A handy collection.

13. SEIDEL, MICHAEL, *Satiric Inheritance: Rabelais to Sterne* (Princeton: Princeton University Press, 1979). The opening chapters deal with the general concept of satiric inheritance; there is then a series of pieces on selected texts to illuminate the variety of satire. The final essay on *Tristram Shandy* (pp. 250–62) is a rather cursory treatment of the application of the concept of 'gravity'— it is suggested that Toby 'did not know the right side [*sic*] of a woman from the wrong' (p. 257).

14. CHRISTENSEN, INGER, *The Meaning of Metafiction: A Critical Study of Selected Novels by Sterne, Nabokov, Barth and Beckett* (Bergen: Universitetsforlaget, 1981), pp. 15–36. Distracting paragraphing and a rather note-like presentation; explores differences in the characters of Walter and Tristram in relation to their writings and attitudes to the written word, and discusses the reader as *narratee* (i.e. playing a part within the work). For an alternative view of the 'reader' of *Tristram Shandy* see item 17 below.

B. *Tristram Shandy*

15. DONALDSON, IAN, 'Weavers, Gardeners, Gladiators and the Lame: *Tristram Shandy*, viii, 5', *Notes and Queries*, 228 (1983), 61–3. An entertaining discussion of Sterne's sexual allusions in a single chapter of *Tristram Shandy*. A good example of scholarly footnoting increasing one's appreciation.

16. DOHERTY, FRANCES, 'Sterne and Warburton: Another Look', *British Journal for Eighteenth-Century Studies*, 1 (1978), 20–30. Argues that the conventional view of Sterne pillorying Warburton and his work, particularly *The Divine Legation of Moses*, may be mistaken. Should be consulted together with item 21 below.

17. DOWLING, WILLIAM C., 'Tristram Shandy's Phantom Audience', *Novel*, 13 (1979–80), 284–95. Differentiates between the reader addressed in the novel as 'Sir' or 'Madam' and the reader who is holding the book. Develops the argument that the narrator is not Tristram Shandy but an imaginary unnamed Yorkshire clergyman who is using Tristram as a fictive voice. This piece has panache.

18. HOEFNAGEL, DICK, 'Sterne and Avicenna', *Notes and Queries*, 226 (1981), 305. A short note on Sterne's use of a pun in Latin: *de omni*

scribili. A reminder of the intellectual level expected of Sterne's readers. Cf. item 15 above.

19. LAMB, JONATHAN, 'Sterne's Use of Montaigne', *Comparative Literature*, 32, No. 1 (1980), 1–41. An informative, though rather long-winded, account of one of the most important influences on Sterne's style and content.

20. MILLER, J. HILLIS, 'Narrative Middle: a Preliminary Outline', *Genre* 11 (1978), 375–87. *Tristram Shandy* is a comic novel; criticism of it is all too often conspicuously tedious. This is not. J. Hillis Miller is both amusing and intellectually stimulating about the concept of the 'line', pictorial and narrative.

21. NEW, MELVYN, 'Sterne, Warburton, and the Burden of Exuberant Wit', *Eighteenth-Century Studies*, 15 (1982), 245–74. Cf. item 16 above. Melvyn New disagrees almost totally with Frances Doherty, claiming that Sterne saw and took a number of opportunities to snipe at Warburton. This piece is the more convincing of the two.

22. ROSENBLUM, MICHAEL, 'The Sermon, the King of Bohemia, and the Art of Interpolation in *Tristram Shandy*', *Studies in Philology*, 75 (1978), 472–91. Highly entertaining discussion of one of the most important of Sterne's narrative devices.

23. ROSENBLUM, MICHAEL, 'Shandean Geometry and the Challenge of Contingency', *Novel*, 10 (1977), 237–47. An informed and informative discussion about the nature of chance and cause and effect in *Tristram Shandy*.

24. ROUSSEAU, G. S., 'Threshold and Explanation: the Social Anthropologist and the Literary Critic of Eighteenth-Century Literature', *The Eighteenth Century: Theory and Interpretation*, 22 (1981), 127–52. An unnecessarily pretentious title which might lead one to expect a piece by a latter-day Vander Blonederdondergewdenstronke. The second section of the piece, pp. 133–37, is a sensible discussion of Widow Wadman.

25. SINFIELD, MARK, 'Uncle Toby's Potency: some critical and authorial confusions in *Tristram Shandy*', *Notes and Queries*, 223 (1978), 54–5. Points out that an error in Work's edition: 'defended' for 'defeated' in IX, 23, has led critics to misapprehend the nature of Toby's wound, and that this has been further compounded by Sterne's own confusions as a result of the demands of his chronology.

26. SMITTEN, JEFFREY, '*Tristram Shandy* and Spatial Form', *Ariel*, 8, No. 4 (1977), 43–55. Cf. the same author's 'Spatial Form as Narrative Technique in *A Sentimental Journey*', *Journal of Narrative Technique*, 5 (1975), 208–18. The opening couple of pages and the

closing paragraph attempt, unconvincingly, to relate *Tristram Shandy* to Frank's concept of spatial form. The bulk of the essay is a detailed discussion of Volume III, and well done. 'Spatial form' is a red herring.

27. WENDELL, ELIZABETH M., *Der Leser als Protagonist: Didaktische Strukturen in Laurences Sternes Tristram Shandy* (Frankfurt am Main: Peter Lang, 1979). A monograph dealing with Sterne's apparent expectations of the reader, whom he refers to when commenting upon the marbled page as 'unlearned'. Arrives at the unsurprising conclusion that there are few who read *Tristram Shandy* who derive as much from it as Sterne might have wished. On the way there are helpful hints to the reader wishing to order this matter better.

28. ZACH, WOLFGANG, ' "My Uncle Toby's Apologetical Oration" und die politische Sinndimension von *Tristram Shandy*', *Germanisch-Romanische Monatsschrift*, n.s. 27 (1977), 391–416. After initially rehearsing the indebtedness of the 'Oration' to the *Anatomy of Melancholy* and recounting the importance of Tindal's continuation of Rapin's *History of England* to the presentation of Toby's character, Wolfgang Zach proceeds to discuss *Tristram Shandy* in the light of contemporary parliamentary debate over the Seven Years' War. This essay deserves much wider circulation.

C. A Sentimental Journey

29. BATTESTIN, MARTIN C., '*A Sentimental Journey* and the Syntax of Things', in *Augustan Worlds: New Essays in Eighteenth-Century Literature in Honour of A. R. Humphreys*, ed. J. C. Hilson, M. M. B. Jones and J. R. Watson (Leicester: Leicester University Press, 1978). Takes the word *syntax* in both linguistic and metaphysical senses and develops his argument to show the importance to Sterne of the concept of grammar and the value of physical contact to communication. A coherent discussion of the problem of bawdy in Sterne's work with a timely reminder of the importance of *honi soit qui mal y pense*.

30. CHADWICK, JOSEPH, 'Infinite Jest: Interpretation in Sterne's *A Sentimental Journey*', *Eighteenth-Century Studies*, 12 (1978–79), 190–205. A number of passages from *A Sentimental Journey* are discussed in detail and with perception. The emphasis is upon the importance of the syntactic element, and the result is one of the few valuable articles on this novel to have appeared recently.

D. Sermons of Mr. Yorick

31. DOWNEY, JAMES, '*The Sermons of Mr. Yorick*: A Reassessment of Hammond', *English Studies in Canada*, 4 (1978), 193–211. James Downey, who is editing the *Sermons* for the Florida edition, here argues convincingly that Lansing Van der Heyden Hammond's attempt to construct a chronology of Sterne's sermons in *Laurence Sterne's Sermons of Mr. Yorick* (New Haven: Yale University Press, 1948) is flawed.

E. Journal to Eliza

32. VAN LEEWEN, EVA C., *Sterne's 'Journal to Eliza': A Semiological and Linguistic Approach to the Text* (Tubingen: Gunter Narr, 1981). The only detailed discussion of 'Journal to Eliza'. Originally a Cologne University Ph.D. dissertation with the rather more inviting title, '*Laurence Sternes "Journal to Eliza" als Empfindsamer Essay, oder Die Praxis der Kommunikation*' (Laurence Sterne's 'Journal to Eliza' as a Sentimental Essay, or The Practice of Communication). Though at times rather heavy going, the effort is rewarding. Argues that the 'Journal' far from being rambling and sentimental in its worst sense is a carefully controlled piece of writing.

Notes on Contributors

JACQUES A. BERTHOUD, born in the Jura, Switzerland, 1 March 1935, educated in Geneva and Pietermaritzburg, South Africa, and at the University of the Witwatersrand, Johannesburg. Taught in English Departments in Pietermaritzburg (1961–67), Southampton (1967–79), and York (appointed Head of Department, 1980). Most recent book: *Joseph Conrad, the Major Phase* (C.U.P., 1978). Currently editing *Coriolanus* for the New Cambridge Shakespeare. Former British Chairman of Amnesty International.

EDWARD A. BLOOM and LILLIAN D. BLOOM are Professors of English at, respectively, Brown University and Rhode Island College. The former is also one of the founding editors of *Novel: A Forum on Fiction*. Both have been Guggenheim and Huntington Library Fellows and recipients of a Research Grant from the National Endowment for the Humanities. They have published extensively, individually and jointly, in criticism, and on eighteenth-century and American literary subjects. Among their collaborative efforts are: *Willa Cather's Gift of Sympathy, Joseph Addison's Sociable Animal, Satire's Persuasive Voice*; they have edited Fanny Burney's *Evelina, Camilla* and *Journals and Letters* (Vol. 7). At present they are editing the letters of Hester Lynch (Thrale) Piozzi, 1784–1821.

W. G. DAY has been collaborating with Richard Davies and Melvyn New on the annotations to *Tristram Shandy* which will form Volume 3 of the Florida edition of the works of Sterne. He is editing Sterne's minor writings in the same series, and has completed a full length study of Sterne's verbal borrowings in *Tristram Shandy*.

PARK HONAN is American, but holds a London University Ph.D. and the Chair of English and American Literature at Leeds. He has taught at British universities since 1968 and is working on a Jane Austen biography based on MS sources. His books include *Browning's Characters: A Study in Poetic Technique (1961), The Book, the Ring and the Poet: A Biography of Robert Browning* (with William Irvine, 1974), and *Matthew Arnold: A Life* (Weidenfeld, 1981; Harvard paperback, 1983). He is British editor of *Novel: A Forum on Fiction.* He has twice been awarded Guggenheim Fellowships.

ALAN B. HOWES is Professor of English at the University of Michigan, where he has won awards for good teaching and for contributions to the teaching of English. He holds an M.A. from Middlebury College and a Ph.D. from Yale University. He is the author of *Yorick and the Critics*, a study of Sterne's reputation in England from 1760 to 1868, and the editor of the Critical Heritage *Sterne.*

MARK LOVERIDGE was born in Leeds, Yorkshire, in 1951. He received both his B.A. and his Ph.D from Clare College, Cambridge, and his doctoral thesis was subsequently published as *Laurence Sterne and the Argument About Design.* He is a lecturer in the English department of University College, Swansea, and is married with one son and one daughter.

VALERIE GROSVENOR MYER has taught literature for several Cambridge colleges and published books on Jane Austen and Margaret Drabble, as well as essays, reviews, short stories and poems. In 1983 she chaired the Sterne session at the annual meeting of the Canadian Society for Eighteenth Century Studies at the University of New Brunswick. She is a contributor to the new *Oxford Companion to English Literature* and is currently editing a book on Samuel Richardson for the Critical Studies series.

MELVYN NEW is Professor of English and Chairman of the Department of English, University of Florida. He is the author of *Laurence Sterne as Satirist: A Reading of Tristram Shandy* (1969), co-editor (with Joan New) of *Tristram Shandy: The Text*, 2 vols. (1978) and editor (with W. G. Day and Richard Davies) of *Tristram Shandy: Annotations* (1984), Vols. 1–3 in the Florida Edition of the Works of Laurence Sterne. His articles on Sterne have appeared in *M.L.Q., S.E.L., P.M.L.A., E.C.S., P.B.S.A., S.B.*, and elsewhere.

ROY PORTER is lecturer at the Wellcome Institute for the History of Medicine, 183 Euston Road, London NW1 2BP. His early research in Cambridge, first at Christ's College and later at Churchill College, was in the history of science, particularly geology. He has now moved on to the history of madness and of psychiatry, and has a general interest in English social history. He is author of *English Society in the Eighteenth Century* (Penguin, 1982).

Notes on Contributors

K. G. SIMPSON was born in Ayrshire and is a graduate of Glasgow University. At present he is a lecturer in the Department of English Studies at the University of Strathclyde and specializes in the teaching of the development of the novel and the literature of the period 1900–50. He has published articles on Smollett, Galt, Stevenson, Burns and Sterne, and he is currently completing a study of the Scottish experience of the movement of ideas in the eighteenth century. He is also editing a collection of critical essays on Fielding for the Critical Studies series.

BRUCE STOVEL is Chairman of the English Department at Dalhousie University in Halifax, Nova Scotia. He has a B.A. from Concordia University in Montreal, an Honours B.A. from Pembroke College, Cambridge, and a Ph.D. from Harvard University. After teaching for five years at Yale University, he came to Dalhousie in 1975. He has written essays on Chaucer, Fielding, Jane Austen, Evelyn Waugh and Kingsley Amis, among others, and is currently working on a book on comedy in English literature.

Index

Index

Index